Reactive Programming with RxJS 5

Untangle Your Asynchronous JavaScript Code

Sergi Mansilla

T0256658

The Pragmatic Bookshelf

Raleigh, North Carolina

Many of the designations used by manufacturers and sellers to distinguish their products are claimed as trademarks. Where those designations appear in this book, and The Pragmatic Programmers, LLC was aware of a trademark claim, the designations have been printed in initial capital letters or in all capitals. The Pragmatic Starter Kit, The Pragmatic Programmer, Pragmatic Programming, Pragmatic Bookshelf, PragProg and the linking *g* device are trademarks of The Pragmatic Programmers, LLC.

Every precaution was taken in the preparation of this book. However, the publisher assumes no responsibility for errors or omissions, or for damages that may result from the use of information (including program listings) contained herein.

Our Pragmatic books, screencasts, and audio books can help you and your team create better software and have more fun. Visit us at *https://pragprog.com*.

The team that produced this book includes:

Publisher: Andy Hunt
VP of Operations: Janet Furlow
Managing Editor: Brian MacDonald
Supervising Editor: Jacquelyn Carter
Indexing: Potomac Indexing, LLC
Copy Editor: Jasmine Kwityn
Layout: Gilson Graphics

For sales, volume licensing, and support, please contact *support@pragprog.com*.

For international rights, please contact *rights@pragprog.com*.

Per a tu, Pipus. T'estimo.

Contents

Acknowledgments

I have so many people to thank. There are those who have helped shape the book and those who have helped shape me as a person. I couldn't have done this without any of them. I would particularly like to thank the following:

The exceptional people who came up with the Reactive Extensions library in the first place, and the ones who expanded and evangelized it. This book would obviously not exist without you: Erik Meijer, Matt Podwysocki, Bart De Smet, Wes Dyer, Jafar Husain, André Staltz, and many more I am forgetting.

The folks at The Pragmatic Bookshelf. It has been a pleasure to work with you. Special thanks to Susannah Pfalzer, who has believed in the book since it was nothing but an idea. I was also lucky to get Rebecca Gulick and Brian MacDonald as my editors: you have been professional, (very!) patient, and attentive to my questions. I've been a fan of Pragmatic's books for a long time, and it has been a privilege to write a PragProg book myself. And, yes, both publishers, Dave Thomas and Andy Hunt, do read and review every book!

The brilliant technical reviewers. Stefan Turalski, Tibor Simic, Martijn Reuvers, Randall Koutnik, David Bock, Javier Collado Cabeza, Fred Daoud, Irakli Gozalishvili, Zef Hemel, Ramaninder Singh Jhajj, Aaron Kalair, Daniel Lamb, Brian Schau, and Stephen Wolff, as well as Pragmatic publishers Dave and Andy: this book is infinitely better thanks to all of you. You each selflessly put time and energy into reviewing this book, detecting complicated errors and saving me from more than one embarrassing mistake. Any errors remaining in the book are my own fault.

The friends who are always there, no matter the time and the distance; you know who you are. Thanks for the laughs, the support, the love.

My parents, Narcís and Joana. You never ceased to believe in me and always encouraged me to take on bigger challenges. You bought me my first computer at a time when you struggled to pay the bills. That started it all, and I owe you everything.

My two sons, Adrià and Julian. You were both born while I was writing this book (first and second editions!), and you have changed the meaning of life for me. You've already taught me so much in such little time. It's a privilege to spend time with you and to witness how you grow up.

Finally, Jen, the love of my life. You were endlessly patient and supportive while I wrote a book during one of the busiest periods of our life. You are an inspiration to me and you make me a better human being. You are my star.

Sergi Mansilla
Barcelona, February 2018

Preface

Reactive programming is taking the software world by storm. This book combines the reactive programming philosophy with the possibilities of JavaScript, and you'll learn how to apply reactive techniques to your own projects. We'll focus on reactive programming to manage and combine streams of events. In fact, we'll cover how to make entire real-world, concurrent applications just by declaring transformations on our program's events.

Most software today deals with data that's available only over time: websites load remote resources and respond to complex user interactions, servers are distributed across multiple physical locations, and people have mobile devices that they expect to work at all times, whether on high-speed Wi-Fi or spotty cellular networks. Any serious application involves many moving asynchronous parts that need to be efficiently coordinated, and that's very hard with today's programming techniques. On top of that, we have what's always been there: servers crashing, slow networks, and software bugs we have to deal with.

We can't afford to keep programming applications the way we always have. It worked for a while, but now it's time for a new approach.

New World, Old Methods

In recent years JavaScript has become the most ubiquitous language in the world and now powers the mission-critical infrastructure of businesses such as Walmart and Netflix,[1] mobile operating systems such as Firefox OS, and complex popular applications such as Google Docs.

And yet we're still using good ol' imperative-style programming to deal with problems that are essentially asynchronous. This is very hard.

JavaScript developers see the language's lack of threads as a feature, and we usually write asynchronous code using callbacks, promises, and events. But

---

1. http://venturebeat.com/2012/01/24/why-walmart-is-using-node-js/, http://techblog.netflix.com/2014/06/scale-and-performance-of-large.html

as we keep adding more concurrency to our applications, the code to coordinate asynchronous flows becomes unwieldy. Current mechanisms all have serious shortcomings that hinder the developer's productivity and make for fragile applications.

Here's a quick rundown of the current mechanisms for handling asynchronous operations, along with their problems.

Callback Functions

A *callback* is a function *(A)* passed as a parameter to another function *(B)* that performs an asynchronous operation. When *(B)* is done, it *calls back (A)* with the results of the operation. Callbacks are used to manage asynchronous flows such as network I/O, database access, or user input.

```
intro/callback_example.js
function B(callback) {
  // Do operation that takes some time
  callback('Done!');
}

function A(message) {
  console.log(message);
}

// Execute `B` with `A` as a callback
B(A);
```

Callbacks are easy to grasp and have become the default way of handling asynchronous data flows in JavaScript. But this simplicity comes at a price. Callbacks have the following drawbacks:

- *Callback hell.* It's easy to end up with lots of nested callbacks when handling highly asynchronous code. When that happens, code stops being linear and becomes hard to reason about. Whole applications end up passed around in callbacks, and they become difficult to maintain and debug.

- *Callbacks can run more than once.* There's no guarantee the same callback will be called only once. Multiple invocations can be hard to detect and can result in errors and general mayhem in your application.

- *Callbacks change error semantics.* Callbacks break the traditional *try/catch* mechanism and rely on the programmer to check for errors and pass them around.

- *Concurrency gets increasingly complicated.* Combining interdependent results of multiple asynchronous operations becomes difficult. It requires us to keep track of the state of each operation in temporal variables, and then delegate them to the final combination operation in the proper order.

Promises

Promises came to save us from callbacks. A promise represents the result of an asynchronous operation. In promise-based code, calling an asynchronous function immediately returns a "promise" that will eventually be either *resolved* with the result of the operation or *rejected* with an error. In the meantime, the *pending* promise can be used as a placeholder for the final value.

Promises usually make programs more clear by being closer to synchronous code, reducing the need for nesting blocks and keeping track of less state.

Unfortunately, promises are not a silver bullet. They're an improvement over callbacks, but they have a major shortcoming: they only ever yield a single value. That makes them useless for handling recurrent events such as mouse clicks or streams of data coming from the server, because we would have to create a promise for each separate event instead of creating a promise that handles the stream of events as it comes.

Event Emitters

When we emit an event, event listeners that are subscribed to it will fire. Using events is a great way to decouple functionality, and in JavaScript, event programming is common and generally a good practice.

But, you guessed it, event listeners come with their own set of problems, too:

- *Events force side effects*. Event listener functions always ignore their return values, which forces the listener to have side effects if it wants to have any impact in the world.

- *Events are not first-class values*. For example, a series of click events can't be passed as a parameter or manipulated as the sequence it actually is. We're limited to handling each event individually, and only after the event happens.

- *It is easy to miss events if we start listening too late*. An infamous example of that is the first version of the *streams* interface in Node.js, which would often emit its data event before listeners had time to listen to it, losing it forever.

Since these mechanisms are what we've always used to manage concurrency, it might be hard to think of a better way. But in this book I'll show you one:

reactive programming and RxJS try to solve all these problems with some new concepts and mechanisms to make asynchronous programming a breeze —and much more fun.

What Is Reactive Programming?

Reactive programming is a programming paradigm that encompasses many concepts and techniques. In this book I'll focus particularly on creating, transforming, and reacting to streams of data. Mouse clicks, network requests, arrays of strings—all these can be expressed as streams to which we can "react" as they publish new values, using the same interfaces regardless of their source.

Reactive programming focuses on propagating changes without our having to explicitly specify how the propagation happens. This allows us to state what our code should do, without having to code every step to do it. This results in a more reliable and maintainable approach to building software.

What Is RxJS?

RxJS is a JavaScript implementation of the Reactive Extensions, or Rx.[2] Rx is a reactive programming model originally created at Microsoft that allows developers to easily compose asynchronous streams of data. It provides a common interface to combine and transform data from wildly different sources, such as filesystem operations, user interaction, and social-network updates.

Rx started with an implementation for .NET, but today it has a well-maintained open source implementation in every major language (and some minor ones). It is becoming the standard to program reactive applications, and Rx's main data type, the Observable, is being proposed for inclusion in ECMAScript 7 as an integral part of JavaScript.

Who This Book Is For

This book is for developers with some experience with JavaScript. You should be comfortable with closures and higher-order functions, and you should understand the scope rules in JavaScript. That being said, I try to explain the most complex language concepts we go through in this book.

What's in This Book

This book is a practical introduction to reactive programming using RxJS. The objective is to get you to think reactively by building small real-world

---

2.   https://rx.codeplex.com/

applications, so you can learn how to introduce reactive programming in your day-to-day programming and make your programs more robust. This is not a theoretical book about reactive programming, and it is not an exhaustive reference book for the RxJS API. You can find these kinds of resources online.

We'll be developing mostly for the browser, but we'll see some examples in Node.js, too. We'll get deep into the subject early on, and we'll build applications along the way to keep it real. Here are the chapters:

- Unless you have used RxJS before, start with Chapter 1, *The Reactive Way*, on page 1. In this chapter we introduce Observables, the main data type of RxJS, which we'll use extensively throughout the book.

- With the basics of Observables established, we move on to Chapter 2, *Deep in the Sequence*, on page 17. There you see that in reactive programming it's all about sequences of events. We visit some important sequence operators and we build our first application, a real-time earthquake visualizer.

- In Chapter 3, *Building Concurrent Programs*, on page 39, we look at how to write concurrent code with minimal side effects. After covering the Observable pipeline, we build a cool spaceship video game in about 200 lines of code and with almost no global state.

- In Chapter 4, *Building a Complete Web Application*, on page 69, we get deeper into reactive app development and enhance the earthquake application we made previously in Chapter 2 on page 17 by making a server part in Node.js that shows tweets related to earthquakes happening right now.

- We get into some more advanced concepts of RxJS with Chapter 5, *Bending Time with Schedulers*, on page 89, where we talk about the useful concept RxJS provides to handle concurrency at a more fine-grained level: Schedulers.

- With the knowledge of Schedulers under our hats, we explore how they help us with testing. We'll see how to simulate time in our tests to accurately test asynchronous programs.

- Finally, in Chapter 6, *Reactive Web Applications with Cycle.js*, on page 101, we'll use Cycle.js, a UI framework built on top of RxJS, to build a simple application. Cycle.js draws concepts from modern frameworks such as React.js to create a reactive framework that uses the advantages of Observables to help us create fast user interfaces in a simple and reliable way.

Running the Code Examples

The code examples in this book are made for either the browser or Node.js. The context of the code should clarify in what environment to run the code.

Running RxJS Code in the Browser

Although we could include a minified RxJS library directly in an HTML page by using a <script> tag and it would work for simple code, it would eventually complicate things when we start using ES6 in our code, which RxJS5 encourages. This is because we can't count on all browsers to understand the complete ES6 syntax, especially when we import modules. If you still want to simply import RxJS directly in an HTML page, it is advised that you use a CDN like unpkg,[3] in which you can import the entire RxJS library already minified.

The easiest way to run RxJS 5 code for the browser is by using a module bundler like Webpack that takes our ES6 source code and compiles it into compatible JavaScript, using the modules we require in the code. That also provides us with a rapid development environment in which any changes in the code are immediately reflected in the running application.

Learning how to configure a module bundler such as Webpack is beyond the scope of this book, but if you want to just start coding without worrying about module bundlers, you can use the Webpack boilerplate project I made from my GitHub repository.[4]

Running RxJS Code in Node.js

Running code examples in Node.js is easy. Just make sure you install the RxJS dependency in your project using npm:

```
$ npm install rxjs
+ rxjs@5.4.2
added 2 packages in 2.674s
```

After that, you can import the RxJS library in your JavaScript files:

```
const Rx = require('rxjs/Rx');

Rx.Observable.of(1,2,3).subscribe(value => {
  console.log(value);
});
```

---

3. https://unpkg.com/rxjs/bundles/Rx.min.js
4. https://github.com/sergi/rxjs-minimal-boilerplate

The preceding code would import the whole Rx library. If don't need all the bells and whistles the library provides, you could import only the necessary code to use the Observable.of operator for our example:

```
const Observable = require('rxjs/Observable').Observable;

Observable.of(1,2,3).subscribe(value => {
  console.log(value);
});
```

And you can run it by simply invoking node and the name of the file:

```
$ node test.js
1
2
3
```

RxJS Version

At the time of writing, the current RxJS version is 5.5.0. All the examples in this book are made for RxJS 5.x.

Resources

RxJS is gaining adoption very quickly, and there are more and more resources about it every day. At times it might be hard to find resources about it online, though. Here are some good ones:

- RxJS5 official source code repository[5]

- ReactiveX, a collection of resources and documentation related to the Reactive Extensions, in several programming languages[6]

- RxMarbles, an interactive tool to visualize Observables[7]

- RxVisualizer, an animated playground for Rx Observables[8]

Download Sample Code

This book's website has links to an interactive discussion forum as well as a place to submit errata.[9] You'll also find the source code for all the projects we build. Readers of the ebook can interact with the box above each code snippet to view that snippet directly.

---

5. https://github.com/ReactiveX/RxJS

6. http://reactivex.io

7. http://rxmarbles.com/

8. https://rxviz.com/

9. http://pragprog.com/titles/smreactjs

CHAPTER 1

The Reactive Way

The real world is pretty messy: events happen in random order, applications crash, and networks fail. Few applications are completely synchronous, and writing asynchronous code is necessary to keep applications responsive. Most of the time it's downright painful, but it really doesn't have to be.

Modern applications need super-fast responses and the ability to process data from different sources at the same time without missing a beat. Current techniques won't get us there because they don't scale—code becomes exponentially more complex as we add concurrency and application state. They get the job done only at the expense of a considerable mental load on the developer, and that leads to bugs and complexity in our code.

This chapter introduces you to reactive programming, a natural, easier way to think about asynchronous code. I'll show you how streams of events—which we call *Observables*—are a beautiful way to handle asynchronous code. Then we'll create an Observable and see how reactive thinking and RxJS dramatically improve on existing techniques and make you a happier, more productive programmer.

What's Reactive?

Let's start by looking at a little program. This program retrieves data from different sources with the click of a button. It has the following requirements:

- It must unify data from two different locations that use different JSON structures.

- The final result should not contain any duplicates.

- The user should not be able to click the button more than once every second, to avoid requesting data too many times.

Using RxJS, we would write something like this:

```
import { Observable } from "rxjs";

const button = document.getElementById("retrieveDataBtn");
const source1 = Observable.ajax.getJSON("/resource1").pluck("name");
const source2 = Observable.ajax.getJSON("/resource2").pluck("props", "name");

const getResults = amount =>
  source1
    .merge(source2)
    .pluck("names")
    .flatMap(array => Observable.from(array))
    .distinct()
    .take(amount);

const clicks = Observable.fromEvent(button, "click");

clicks
  .debounceTime(1000)
  .flatMap(getResults(5))
  .subscribe(
    value => console.log("Received value", value),
    err => console.error(err),
    () => console.log("All values retrieved!")
  );
```

Don't worry about understanding what's going on here; let's focus on the 10,000-foot view for now. The first thing you see is that we express a lot with very few lines of code. We accomplish this by using Observables.

An Observable represents a stream of data. Programs can be expressed largely as streams of data. In the preceding example, both remote sources are Observables, and so are the mouse clicks from the user. In fact, our program is essentially a single Observable made from a button's click event that we transform to get the results we want.

Reactive programming is expressive. Take, for instance, throttling mouse clicks in our example. Imagine how complex it would be to do that using callbacks or promises: we'd need to reset a timer every second and keep state of whether a second has passed since the last time the user clicked the button. It's a lot of complexity for such little functionality, and the code needed for it is not even related to the program's actual functionality. In bigger applications, these complexities add up very quickly to make for a tangled code base.

With the reactive approach, we use the method debounce to throttle the stream of clicks. This ensures that there is at least a second between each click, and discards any clicks in between. We don't care how this happens internally; we just express *what* we want our code to do, and not *how* to do it.

It gets much more interesting. Next you'll see how reactive programming can help us make our programs more efficient and expressive.

Spreadsheets Are Reactive

Let's start by considering the quintessential example of a reactive system: the spreadsheet. We all have used them, but we rarely stop and think how shockingly intuitive they are. Let's say we have a value in cell A1 of the spreadsheet. We can then reference it in other cells in the spreadsheet, and whenever we change A1, every cell depending on A1 will automatically update its own value.

B1			f_x Σ $=$	$=A1/5$
		A	B	C
1		100	20	500
2				

That behavior feels natural to us. We didn't have to tell the computer to update cells that depend on A1 or how to do it; these cells just *reacted* to the change. In a spreadsheet, we simply *declare* our problem, and we don't worry about how the computer calculates the results.

This is what reactive programming aims for. We declare relationships between entities, and the program evolves as these entities change.

The Mouse as a Stream of Values

To understand how to see events as streams of values, let's revisit the program from the beginning of this chapter. There we used mouse clicks as an infinite sequence of values generated in real time as the user clicks. This is an idea proposed by Erik Meijer—the inventor of RxJS—in his paper "Your Mouse Is a Database."[1]

In reactive programming, we see mouse clicks as a continuous stream of values that we can query and manipulate. Thinking about a stream of values instead of discrete values opens up a whole new way to program, one in which we can manipulate entire sequences of values that haven't been created yet.

Let that thought sink in for a moment. This is different from what we're used to, which is having values stored somewhere such as a database or an array, and waiting for them to be available before we use them. If they are not available yet (for instance, a network request), we wait for them and use them only when they become available.

---

1. http://queue.acm.org/detail.cfm?id=2169076

We can think of our stream as an array in which elements are separated by *time* instead of by memory. With either time or memory, we have a sequence of elements:

Seeing your program as sequences of data is key to understanding RxJS programming. It takes a bit of practice, but it is not hard. In fact, most data we use in any application can be expressed as a sequence. We'll look at sequences in more depth in Chapter 2, *Deep in the Sequence*, on page 17.

Querying the Sequence

Let's implement a simple version of that mouse stream using traditional event listeners in JavaScript. To log the x- and y-coordinates of mouse clicks, we could write something like this:

ch1/thinking_sequences.js
```
const registerClicks = e => {
  console.log(e.clientX, e.clientY);
};
document.body.addEventListener("click", registerClicks);
```

This code will print the x- and y-coordinates of every mouse click in order. The output looks like this:

```
252  183
211  232
153  323
...
```

Looks like a sequence, doesn't it? The problem, of course, is that manipulating events is not as easy as manipulating arrays. For example, if we want to change the preceding code so it logs only the first 10 clicks that happen on the right side of the screen (quite a random goal, but bear with me here), we would write something like this:

```
let clicks = 0;
document.addEventListener("click", e => {
  if (clicks < 10) {
    if (e.clientX > window.innerWidth / 2) {
      console.log(e.clientX, e.clientY);
      clicks += 1;
    }
  } else {
    document.removeEventListener("click", registerClicks);
  }
});
```

To meet our requirements, we introduced external state through a global variable clicks that counts clicks made so far. We also need to check for two different conditions and use nested conditional blocks. And when we're done, we have to tidy up and unregister the event to not leak memory.

Side Effects and External State

If an action has impact outside of the scope where it happens, we call this a *side effect*. Changing a variable external to our function, printing to the console, or updating a value in a database are examples of side effects.

For example, changing the value of a variable that exists *inside* our function is safe. But if that variable is *outside* the scope of our function then other functions can change its value. That means our function is not in control anymore and it can't assume that external variable contains the value we expect. We'd need to track it and add checks to ensure its value is what we expect. At that point we'd be adding code that is not relevant to our program, making it more complex and error prone.

Although side effects are necessary to build any interesting program, we should strive for having as few as possible in our code. That's especially important in reactive programs, where we have many moving pieces that change over time. Throughout this book, we'll pursue an approach that avoids external state and side effects. In fact, in Chapter 3, *Building Concurrent Programs*, on page 39, we'll build an entire video game with no side effects.

We managed to meet our easy requirements, but ended up with pretty complicated code for such a simple goal. The code is not obvious for a developer who looks at it for the first time. More importantly, we made it easier to introduce subtle bugs in the future because we need to keep state.

If we think about it, all we want to do is to query a "database" of clicks. If we were dealing with a relational database, we'd use the declarative language SQL to write something similar to this:

```
SELECT x, y FROM clicks LIMIT 10
```

What if we treated that stream of click values as a database that can be queried? After all, it's no different from a database, one that emits values in real time. All we need is a data type that abstracts the concept for us.

Enter RxJS and its Observable data type:

```
Observable.fromEvent(document, "click")
  .filter(c => c.clientX > window.innerWidth / 2)
  .take(10)
  .subscribe(c => console.log(c.clientX, c.clientY));
```

This code does the same as the code on page 5, and it reads like this:

> Create an Observable of click events and filter out the clicks that happen on the left side of the screen. Then print the coordinates of only the first 10 clicks to the console as they happen.

Notice how the code is easy to read even if you're not familiar with it. Also, there's no need to create external variables to keep state, which makes the code self-contained and makes it harder to introduce bugs. There's no need to clean up after yourself either, so no chance of introducing memory leaks by forgetting about unregistering event handlers.

In the preceding code we created an Observable from a DOM event. An Observable provides us with a stream of values that we can manipulate as a whole instead of handling a single isolated event each time. Dealing with sequences gives us enormous power; we can merge, transform, or pass around Observables easily. We've turned events we can't get a handle on into a tangible data structure that's as easy to use as an array, but much more flexible.

In the next section we'll see the principles that make Observables such a great tool.

Observers and Iterators

To understand where Observables come from we need to look at their foundations: the Observer and Iterator software patterns. In this section we'll take a quick look at them, and then we'll see how Observables combine concepts of both in a simple but powerful way.

The Observer Pattern

For a software developer, it's hard to hear about Observables and not think of the venerable Observer pattern. In it we have an object called *Producer* that keeps an internal list of *Listeners* subscribed to it. Listeners are notified—by calling their update method—whenever the state of the Producer changes. (In most explanations of the Observer pattern, this entity is called *Subject*, but to avoid confusion with RxJS's own *Subject* type, we call it *Producer*.)

It's easy to implement a rudimentary version of the pattern in a few lines:

ch1/observer_pattern.js
```js
class Producer {
  constructor() {
    this.listeners = [];
  }

  add(listener) {
    this.listeners.push(listener);
  }

  remove(listener) {
    const index = this.listeners.indexOf(listener);
    this.listeners.splice(index, 1);
  }

  notify(message) {
    this.listeners.forEach(listener => {
      listener.update(message);
    });
  }
}
```

The Producer object keeps a list of Listeners in the instance's listeners array that will all be updated whenever the Producer calls its notify method. In the following code we create two objects that listen to notifier, an instance of Producer:

ch1/observer_pattern.js
```js
// Any object with an 'update' method would work.
const listener1 = {
  update: message => {
    console.log("Listener 1 received:", message);
  }
};

const listener2 = {
  update: message => {
    console.log("Listener 2 received:", message);
  }
};

const notifier = new Producer();
notifier.add(listener1);
notifier.add(listener2);
notifier.notify("Hello there!");
```

When we run the program

```
Listener 1 received: Hello there!
Listener 2 received: Hello there!
```

listener1 and listener2 are notified whenever the Producer notifier updates its internal state, without us having to check for it.

Our implementation is simple, but it illustrates how the Observer pattern allows decoupling between the events and the listener objects that react to them.

The Iterator Pattern

The other piece in the Observable puzzle comes from the Iterator pattern. An Iterator is an object that provides a consumer with an easy way to traverse its contents, hiding the implementation from the consumer.

The Iterator interface is simple. It requires only two methods: next() to get the next item in the sequence, and hasNext() to check if there are items left in the sequence.

Here's how we'd write an iterator that operates on an array of numbers and yields only elements that are multiples of the divisor parameter:

```
ch1/iterator.js
class MultipleIterator {
  constructor(arr, divisor = 1) {
    this.cursor = 0;
    this.array = arr;
    this.divisor = divisor;
  }

  next() {
    while (this.cursor < this.array.length) {
      const value = this.array[this.cursor++];
      if (value % this.divisor === 0) {
        return value;
      }
    }
  }

  hasNext() {
    let cur = this.cursor;
    while (cur < this.array.length) {
      if (this.array[cur++] % this.divisor === 0) {
        return true;
      }
    }
    return false;
  }
}
```

We can use this iterator like this:

```
ch1/iterator.js
const consumer = new iterateOnMultiples(
  [1, 2, 3, 4, 5, 6, 7, 8, 9, 10],
  3
);

console.log(consumer.next(), consumer.hasNext()); // 3 true
console.log(consumer.next(), consumer.hasNext()); // 6 true
console.log(consumer.next(), consumer.hasNext()); // 9 false
```

Iterators offer a great way to encapsulate traversing logic for any kind of data structure. As we saw in the preceding example, iterators get interesting when made generic to handle different types of data, or when they can be configured in runtime, like we did in our example with the divisor parameter.

The Rx Pattern and the Observable

While the Observer and the Iterator patterns are powerful in their own right, the combination of both is even better. We call this the Rx pattern, named after the Reactive Extensions libraries.[2] We'll be using this pattern for the rest of the book.

The *Observable sequence*, or simply *Observable* is central to the Rx pattern. An Observable emits its values in order—like an iterator—but instead of its consumers requesting the next value, the Observable "pushes" values to consumers as they become available. It has a similar role to the Producer's in the Observer pattern: emitting values and pushing them to its listeners.

Pulling vs. Pushing

In programming, *push-based behavior* means that the server component of an application sends updates to its clients instead of the clients having to poll the server for these updates. It's like the saying, "Don't call us; we'll call you."

RxJS is push-based, so the source of events (the Observable) will push new values to the consumer (the Subscriber), without the consumer requesting the next value.

Put more simply, an Observable is a sequence whose items become available over time. The consumers of Observables, Subscriptions, are the equivalent of *listeners* in the Observer pattern. When a Subscription subscribes to an Observable, it receives the values in the sequence as they become available, without having to request them.

---

2. https://rx.codeplex.com/

So far it doesn't seem very different from the traditional Observer pattern. But actually there are two essential differences:

- An Observable doesn't start streaming items until it has at least one Observer subscribed to it.

- Like iterators, an Observable can signal when the sequence is completed.

Using Observables, we can declare how to react to the sequence of elements, instead of reacting to individual items. We can efficiently copy, transform, and query the sequence, and these operations will apply to all the elements of the sequence.

Creating Observables

There are several ways to create Observables, the create operator being the most obvious one. The create operator in the Rx.Observable object takes a callback that accepts an Observer as a parameter. That function defines how the Observable will emit values. Here's how we create a simple Observable:

```
const observable = Observable.create(observer => {
  observer.next("Simon");
  observer.next("Jen");
  observer.next("Sergi");
  observer.complete(); // We are done
});
```

When we subscribe to this Observable, it emits three strings by calling the next method on its listeners. It then calls complete to signal that the sequence is finished. But how exactly do we subscribe to an Observable? We use Observers.

The Observer Interface

Whenever an event happens in an Observable, it calls the related method in all of its Subscribers. Subscribers have to implement the *Observer interface*.

The Observer interface contains three methods: next, complete, and error:

next The equivalent of Update in the Observer pattern. It is called when the Observable emits a new value. Notice how the name reflects the fact that we're subscribed to sequences, not only to discrete values.

complete Signals that there is no more data available. After complete is called, further calls to next will have no effect.

error Called when an error occurs in the Observable. After it is called, further calls to next will have no effect.

Here's how we create a basic Observer from scratch:

```
const subscriber = Subscriber.create(
  value => console.log(`Next: ${value}`),
  error => console.log(`Error: ${error}`),
  () => console.log("Completed")
);
```

The create method in the Rx.Subscriber class takes functions for the next, complete, and error cases and returns a Subscriber instance. These three functions are optional, and you can decide which ones to include. For example, if we are subscribing to an infinite sequence such as clicks on a button (the user could keep clicking forever), the complete handler will never be called. If we're confident that the sequence can't error (for example, by making an Observable from an array of numbers), we don't need the error method.

Making Ajax Calls with an Observable

We haven't done anything really useful with Observables yet. How about creating an Observable that retrieves remote content? To do this, we'll wrap the XMLHttpRequest object using Rx.Observable.create:

```
function get(url) {
  return Observable.create(subscriber => {
    // Make a traditional Ajax request
    const req = new XMLHttpRequest();
    req.open("GET", url);

    req.onload = () => {
      if (req.status === 200) {
        // If the status is 200, meaning there have been no problems,
        // yield the result to listeners and complete the sequence
        subscriber.next(req.response);
        subscriber.complete();
      } else {
        // Otherwise, signal to listeners that there has been an error
        subscriber.error(new Error(req.statusText));
      }
    };

    req.onerror = () => {
      subscriber.error(new Error("Unknown Error"));
    };

    req.send();
  });
}

// Create an Ajax Observable
const test = get("/api/contents.json");
```

In the preceding code, the get function uses create to wrap XMLHttpRequest. If the HTTP *GET* request is successful, we emit its contents and complete the sequence (our Observable will only ever emit one result). Otherwise, we emit an error. On the last line we call the function with a particular URL to retrieve. This will create the Observable, but it won't make any request yet. This is important: Observables don't do anything until at least one Observer subscribes to them. So let's take care of that:

```
// Subscribe an Observer to it
test.subscribe(
  value => console.log(`Result: ${value}`),
  error => console.log(`Error: ${error}`),
  () => console.log("Completed")
);
```

The first thing to notice is that we're not explicitly creating a Subscriber like we did in the code on page 11. Most of the time we'll use this shorter version, in which we call the subscribe operator in the Observable with the three functions mandated by the Observer interface: next, complete, and error.

subscribe then sets everything in motion. Before the subscription, we had merely declared how the Observable and Subscriber duo will interact. It is only when we call subscribe that the gears start turning.

There Is (Almost) Always an Operator

In RxJS, methods that transform or query sequences are called *operators*. Operators are found in the static Rx.Observable object and in Observable instances. In our example, create is one such operator.

create is a good choice when we have to create a very specific Observable, but RxJS provides plenty of other operators that make it easy to create Observables for common sources.

Let's look again at our previous example. For such a common operation as an Ajax request there is often an operator ready for us to use. Since we're doing a GET request, we can use the default form of the Rx.Observable.ajax operator, and our code then becomes this:

```
Observable.ajax("/api/contents.json").subscribe(
  data => console.log(data.response),
  err => console.error(err)
);
```

This bit of code does exactly the same as our previous one, but we don't have to create a wrapper around XMLHttpRequest; it's already there. Notice also that this time we omitted the complete callback, because we don't plan to react when the Observable is done. We know that it will yield only one result, and we are already using it in the next callback.

We'll use plenty of convenience operators like this throughout this book. RxJS comes with "batteries included." In fact, that is one of its main strengths.

One Data Type to Rule Them All

In an RxJS program, we should strive to have all data in Observables, not just data that comes from asynchronous sources. Doing that makes it easy to combine data from different origins, like an existing array with the result of a callback, or the result of an XMLHttpRequest with some event triggered by the user.

For example, if we have an array whose items need to be used in combination with data from somewhere else, it's better to make this array into an Observable. (Obviously, if the array is just an intermediate variable that doesn't need to be combined, there is no need to do that.) Throughout the book, you'll learn in which situations it's worth transforming data types into Observables.

RxJS provides operators to create Observables from most JavaScript data types. Let's go over the most common ones, which you'll be using all the time: arrays, events, and callbacks.

Creating Observables from Arrays

We can make any array-like or iterable object into an Observable by using the versatile from operator. from takes an array as a parameter and returns an Observable that emits each of its elements:

```
Observable.from(["Adrià", "Julian", "Jen", "Sergi"]).subscribe(
  x => console.log(`Next: ${x}`),
  err => console.log("Error:", err),
  () => console.log("Completed")
);
```

from is, along with fromEvent, one of the most convenient and frequently used operators in RxJS code.

Creating Observables from JavaScript Events

When we transform an event into an Observable, it becomes a first-class value that can be combined and passed around. For example, here's an Observable that emits the coordinates of the mouse pointer whenever it moves:

```
const allMoves$ = Observable.fromEvent(document, "mousemove");
allMoves$.subscribe(e => console.log(e.clientX, e.clientY));
```

Transforming an event into an Observable unleashes the event from its natural constraints. More importantly, we can create new Observables based on the original ones. The new ones are independent and can be used for different tasks:

```
const movesOnTheRight$ = allMoves$.filter(
  e => e.clientX > window.innerWidth / 2
);

const movesOnTheLeft$ = allMoves$.filter(
  e => e.clientX < window.innerWidth / 2
);

movesOnTheRight$.subscribe(e => {
  console.log("Mouse is on the right:", e.clientX);
});

movesOnTheLeft$.subscribe(e => {
  console.log("Mouse is on the left:", e.clientX);
});
```

In the preceding code, we create two Observables from the original allMoves$ one. These specialized Observables contain only filtered items from the original one: movesOnTheRight$ contains mouse events that happen on the right side of the screen, and movesOnTheLeft$ contains mouse events that happen on the left side. Neither of them modify the original Observable: allMoves$ will keep emitting all mouse moves. Observables are immutable, and every operator applied to them creates a new Observable.

Creating Observables from Callback Functions

Chances are you will have to interact with callback-based code if you use third-party JavaScript libraries. We can transform our callbacks into Observables using two functions, bindCallback and bindNodeCallback. Node.js follows the convention of always invoking the callback function with an error argument first to signal to the callback function that there was a problem. We then use bindNodeCallback to create Observables specifically from Node.js-style callbacks:

```
const Rx = require("rxjs"); // Load RxJS
const fs = require("fs"); // Load Node.js Filesystem module

const Observable = Rx.Observable;
// Create an Observable from the readdir method
const readdir$ = Observable.bindNodeCallback(fs.readdir);

const source$ = readdir$("/Users/sergi"); // Send a delayed message

const subscription = source$.subscribe(
  res => console.log(`List of directories: ${res}`),
  error => console.log(`Error: ${error}`),
  () => console.log("Done!")
);
```

In the preceding code, we make an Observable readdir$ out of Node.js's fs.readdir method. fs.readdir accepts a directory path and a callback function that runs once the directory contents are retrieved.

We use readdir$ with the same arguments we'd pass to the original fs.readdir, minus the callback function. This returns an Observable that will properly use next, error, and complete when we subscribe an Observer to it.

Wrapping Up

In this chapter we explored the reactive approach to programming and saw how RxJS can solve the problems of other methods, such as callbacks or promises, through Observables. Now you understand why Observables are powerful, and you know how to create them. Armed with this foundation, we can now go on to create more interesting reactive programs. The next chapter shows you how to create and compose sequence-based programs that provide a more "Observable" approach to some common scenarios in web development.

CHAPTER 2

Deep in the Sequence

I have childhood memories of playing a puzzle video game in which you had to guide a falling stream of water across the screen using all kinds of tricks. You could split the stream, merge it back later, or use a tilted plank of wood to change their direction. You had to be creative to make the water reach its final goal.

I find a lot of similarities between that game and working with Observable sequences. Observables are just streams of events that we transform, combine, and query. It doesn't matter whether we're dealing with simple Ajax callbacks or processing gigabytes of data in Node.js. The way we declare our flows is the same. Once we think in streams, our programs become simpler.

In this chapter we focus on how to effectively use sequences in our programs. So far we've covered how to create Observables and do simple operations with them. To unleash their power, we have to know to translate our program inputs and outputs into sequences that carry our program flow.

Before we get our hands dirty, we'll meet some of the basic operators that will help us start to manipulate sequences. Then we'll implement a real application that shows earthquakes happening in (almost) real time. Let's get to it!

Visualizing Observables

You're about to learn some of the operators that we'll use most frequently in our RxJS programs. Talking about what operators do to a sequence can feel abstract. To help developers understand operators in an easy way, we'll use a standard visual representation for sequences, called *marble diagrams*. They visually represent data streams, and you will find them in almost every resource for RxJS.

Let's start with the range operator, which returns an Observable that emits all integers within a specified range: Rx.Observable.range(1, 3);

The marble diagram for it looks like this:

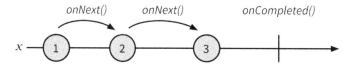

The long arrow represents the Observable, and the x-axis represents time. Each circle represents a value the Observable emits by internally calling next(). After generating the third value, range calls complete, represented in the diagram by a vertical line.

Let's now look at an example that involves several Observables. The merge operator takes two different Observables and returns a new one with the merged values. The interval operator returns an Observable that yields incremental numbers at a given interval of time, expressed in milliseconds.

In the following code we'll merge two different Observables that use interval to produce values at different intervals:

```
const a$ = Observable.interval(200).map(i => `A${i}`);
const b$ = Observable.interval(100).map(i => `B${i}`);

Observable.merge(a$, b$).subscribe(x => {
  console.log(x);
});
```

❮ B0, A0, B1, B2, A1, B3, B4...

The marble diagram for the merge operator looks like this:

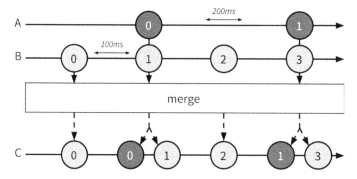

Here, the dotted arrows along the y-axis point to the final result of the transformation applied to each element in sequences A and B. The resulting Observable is represented by C, which contains the merged elements of A and B. If elements of different Observables are emitted at the same time, the order of these elements in the merged sequence is random.

Basic Sequence Operators

Among the dozens of operators that transform Observables in RxJS, the most used are those that any language with decent collection-processing abilities also have: map, filter, and reduce. In JavaScript, you can find these operators in Array instances.

RxJS follows JavaScript conventions, so you'll find that the syntax for the following operators is almost the same as for array operators. In fact, we'll show the implementation using both arrays and Observables to show how similar the two APIs are.

map

map is probably the most used operator. It takes an Observable and a function and applies that function to each of the values in the source Observable. It returns a new Observable with the transformed values.

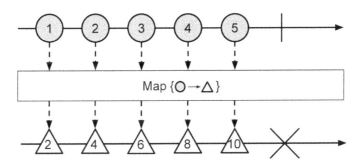

JS Arrays	Observables

```
const src = [1, 2, 3, 4, 5];                 const src = Observable.range(1, 5);
const upper = src.map(name => name * 2);     const upper = src.map(name => name * 2);

upper.forEach(logValue);                     upper.subscribe(logValue);
```

In both cases, src doesn't mutate.

This code, and the code that follows, uses this definition of logValue:

```
function logValue(val) {
  console.log(val);
}
```

It could be that the function we pass to map does some asynchronous computation to transform the value. In that case, map would not work as expected. For these cases, it would be better to use *flatMap*, on page 22.

filter

filter takes an Observable and a function and tests each element in the Observable using that function. It returns an Observable sequence of all the elements for which the function returned true.

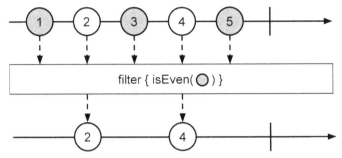

JS Arrays	Observables
`const isEven = val => val % 2 === 0;`	
`const src = [1, 2, 3, 4, 5];` `const even = src.filter(isEven);`	`const src = Observable.range(1, 5);` `const even = src.filter(isEven);`
`even.forEach(logValue);`	`even.subscribe(logValue);`

reduce

reduce (also known as *fold*) takes an Observable and returns a new one that always contains a single item, which is the result of applying a function over each element. That function receives the current element and the result of the function's previous invocation.

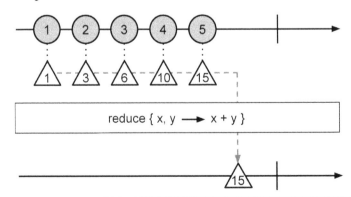

JS Arrays	Observables
`const src = [1, 2, 3, 4, 5];`	`const src = Observable.range(1, 5);`
`const sum = src.reduce((a, b) => a + b);`	`const sum = src.reduce((acc, x) => acc + x);`
`console.log(sum);`	`sum.subscribe(logValue);`

reduce is a crucial operator. It is, in fact, the base implementation for a whole subset of methods called *aggregate operators*.

Aggregate Operators

Aggregate operators process an entire sequence and return a single value. For example, Rx.Observable.first takes an Observable and an optional predicate function and returns the first element that satisfies the condition in the predicate. If there is no predicate function, it just returns the first element in the Observable.

Every aggregate operator can be implemented by using only reduce. Let's take averaging the values of a sequence, for example. RxJS provides the average operator, but for the sake of this section, we want to see how to implement it using reduce:

ch2/1_marble.js
```
const average$ = Observable
  .range(0, 5)
  .reduce(
    (previous, current) => {
      return {
        sum: previous.sum + current,
        count: previous.count + 1
      };
    },
    { sum: 0, count: 0 }
  )
  .map(result => result.sum / result.count);

average$.subscribe(x => console.log("Average is: ", x));
```

‹ Average is: 2

In this code we use reduce to add each new value to the previous one. Because reduce doesn't provide us with the total number of elements in the sequence, we need to keep count of them. We call reduce with an initial value consisting of an object with two fields, sum and count, where we'll store the sum and total count of elements so far. Every new element will return the same object with updated values.

When the sequence ends, reduce will call next with the object containing the final sum and the final count. We then use map to return the result of dividing the sum by the count.

flatMap

What can you do if you have an Observable whose emitted items are more Observables? Most of the time you'd want to merge items in those nested Observables in a single sequence. That's exactly what flatMap does.

The flatMap operator takes an Observable A whose elements are also Observables, and returns an Observable with the flattened values of A's child Observables. Let's visualize it with a graph:

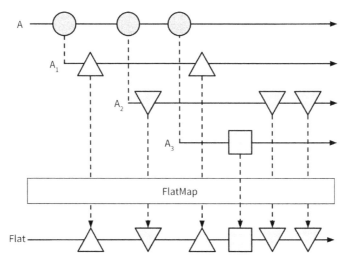

We can see that each of the elements in A (A_1, A_2, A_3) are also Observable sequences. Once we apply flatMap to A with a transformation function, we get an Observable with all the elements in the different children of A.

flatMap is a powerful operator, but it can be harder to understand than the operators we've seen so far. Think of it as a concatAll() for Observables.

concatAll is a function that takes an array of arrays and returns a "flattened" single array containing the values of all the sub-arrays, instead of the sub-arrays themselves. We can use reduce to make such a function:

```
function concatAll(source) {
  return source.reduce((a, b) => a.concat(b));
}
```

We would use it like this:

```
concatAll([[0, 1, 2], [3, 4, 5], [6, 7, 8]]);
// [0, 1, 2, 3, 4, 5, 6, 7, 8]
```

flatMap does the same thing, but it flattens Observables instead of arrays. It takes a source Observable and a function that returns a new Observable and

> ## Joe asks:
> ## Can We Aggregate Infinite Observables?
>
> Imagine we're writing a program that gives users their average speed while they walk. Even if the user hasn't finished walking, we need to be able to make a calculation using the speed values we know so far. We basically want to log the average of an infinite sequence at any given point. The problem is that if the sequence never ends, an aggregate operator like reduce will never call its Subscribers' next operator.
>
> Luckily for us, the RxJS team has thought of this kind of scenario and provided us with the scan operator, which acts like reduce but emits each intermediate result:
>
> ```
> const average$ = Observable.interval(1000)
>   .scan(
>     (previous, current) => {
>       return {
>         sum: previous.sum + current,
>         count: previous.count + 1
>       };
>     },
>     { sum: 0, count: 0 }
>   )
>   .map(result => result.sum / result.count);
> ```
>
> This way, we can aggregate sequences that take a long time to complete or that are infinite. In the preceding example, we generated an incremental integer every second using the interval and substituted the previous reduce call for scan. We now get the average of the values generated so far, every second.

applies that function to each element in the source Observable, like map does. If the process stopped here, we would end up getting an Observable that emits Observables. But flatMap emits to the main sequence the values emitted by each new Observable, "flattening" all Observables into one, the main sequence. In the end, we obtain a single Observable.

This is how we would do the same as concatAll with flatMap:

ch2/3_flatmap.js

```
import { Observable } from 'rxjs';
const values$ = Observable.from([
  Observable.of(1, 2, 3),
  Observable.of(4, 5, 6),
  Observable.of(7, 8, 9)
]);

// values$ is an Observable that emits three Observables

values$.flatMap(v => v).subscribe(v => console.log(v));
```

But as it often happens, RxJS already has an operator for that very purpose named—drum roll, please—concatAll, and makes our code a bit more succinct than flatMap:

```
ch2/4_concatall.js
import { Observable } from "rxjs";
const values$ = Observable.from([
  Observable.of(1, 2, 3),
  Observable.of(4, 5, 6),
  Observable.of(7, 8, 9)
]);

values$.concatAll().subscribe(v => console.log(v));
```

Canceling Sequences

In RxJS we can cancel a running Observable. This is an advantage over other asynchronous forms of communication, such as callbacks and promises, which can't be directly canceled once they're called (some promise implementations support cancellation, though).

There are two main ways we can cancel an Observable: *explicitly* and *implicitly*.

Explicit Cancellation

Observables themselves don't have a method to get canceled. Instead, whenever we subscribe to an Observable we get a Subscription. We can then call the method unsubscribe on the Subscription, and it will stop receiving notifications from the Observable.

In the following example, we subscribe two Observers to the counter Observable, which emits an increasing integer every second. After two seconds, we cancel the second subscription and we can see that its output stops but the first subscriber's output keeps going:

```
ch2/5_disposable.js
import { Observable } from 'rxjs';

const counter$ = Observable.interval(1000);

const subscription1 = counter$.subscribe(i => {
  console.log('Subscription 1:', i);
});

const subscription2 = counter$.subscribe(i => {
  console.log('Subscription 2:', i);
});
```

```
setTimeout(
  () => {
    console.log('Canceling subscription2!');
    subscription2.unsubscribe();
  },
  2000
);
```

```
Subscription 1: 0
Subscription 2: 0
Subscription 1: 1
Subscription 2: 1
Canceling subscription2!
Subscription 1: 2
Subscription 1: 3
Subscription 1: 4
...
```

Implicit Cancellation

Often, operators will cancel subscriptions for you. Operators such as range or take will cancel the subscription when the sequence finishes or when the operator conditions are met. Advanced operators such as withLatestFrom or switchMap will create and destroy subscriptions as needed, since they handle several Observables in motion. In short, don't worry about canceling most subscriptions yourself.

Observables That Wrap External APIs

When you're using Observables that wrap external APIs that don't provide cancellation, the Observable will still stop emitting notifications when canceled, but the underlying API will not necessarily be canceled. For example, if you're using an Observable that wraps a promise, the Observable will stop emitting when canceled, but the underlying promise will not be canceled.

In the following code, we attempt to cancel a subscription to an Observable that wraps a promise p, and at the same time we set an action in the traditional way for when the promise is resolved. The promise should resolve in five seconds, but we cancel the subscription immediately after creating it:

```
const p = new Promise((resolve, reject) => {
  window.setTimeout(resolve, 5000);
});

p.then(() => console.log('Potential side effect!'));

const subscription = Observable
  .fromPromise(p)
  .subscribe(msg => console.log('Observable resolved!'));

subscription.unsubscribe();
```

After five seconds, we see:

```
❰ Potential side effect!
```

If we cancel the subscription to the Observable it effectively stops it from receiving the notification. But the promise's then method still runs, showing that canceling the Observable doesn't cancel the underlying promise.

It's important to know the details of external APIs that we use in Observables. You might think you've canceled a sequence, but the underlying API keeps running and causes some side effects in your program. These errors can be really hard to catch.

Handling Errors

Remember when we talked about the three methods we can call on an Observer? (If you need a refresher, refer back to *The Observer Interface*, on page 10.) We're familiar with next and complete, but we haven't yet used error; it is the key to effectively handling errors in Observable sequences.

To see how it works, we'll write a simple function to take an array of JSON strings and return an Observable that emits the objects parsed from those strings, using JSON.parse:

```
import { Observable } from "rxjs";
function getJSON(arr) {
  return Observable.from(arr).map(JSON.parse);
}
```

We'll pass an array with three JSON strings to getJSON, in which the second string in the array contains a syntax error, so JSON.parse won't be able to parse it. Then we'll subscribe to the result, providing handlers for next and error:

```
getJSON([
  '{"1": 1, "2": 2}',
  '{"success: true}', // Invalid JSON string
  '{"enabled": true}'
]).subscribe(
  json => console.log("Parsed JSON: ", json),
  err => console.log(err.message)
);
```

```
❰ Parsed JSON:  { 1: 1, 2: 2 }
  JSON.parse: unterminated string at line 1 column 8 of the JSON data
```

The Observable emits the parsed JSON for the first result but throws an exception when trying to parse the second. The error handler catches this and prints it out. The default behavior is that whenever an error happens, the Observable stops emitting items, and complete is not called.

Catching Errors

So far we've seen how to detect that an error has happened and do something with that information, but we haven't been able to react to it and continue with whatever we were doing. Observable instances have the catch operator, which allows us to react to an error in the Observable and continue with another Observable.

catch takes either an Observable or a function that receives the error as a parameter and returns another Observable. In our scenario, we want the Observable to emit a JSON object containing an error property if there were errors in the original Observable:

```
function getJSON(arr) {
  return Observable.from(arr).map(JSON.parse);
}
const caught$ = getJSON(['{"1": 1, "2": 2}', '{"1: 1}']).catch(
  Observable.of({
    error: "There was an error parsing JSON"
  })
);

caught$.subscribe(
  json => console.log("Parsed JSON: ", json),
  err => console.log(err.message)
);
```

In the preceding code, we create a new Observable, caught, that uses the catch operator to catch errors in the original Observable. If there's an error it will continue the sequence with an Observable that emits only one item, with an error property describing the error. This is the output:

```
Parsed JSON: Object { 1: 1, 2: 2 }
Parsed JSON: Object { error: "There was an error parsing JSON" }
```

You can see the marble diagram for the catch operator in the figure on page 28.

Notice the X to indicate that the sequence experienced an error. The different shape of the Observable values—triangles in this case—means that they are values coming from another Observable. Here, that's the Observable we return in case of an error.

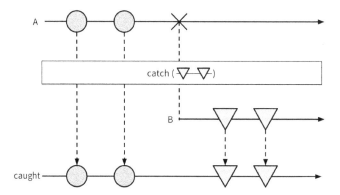

catch is useful for reacting to errors in a sequence, and it behaves much like the traditional try/catch block. In some cases, though, it would be very convenient to ignore an error that happens with an item in the Observable and let the sequence continue. In those cases, we can use the retry operator.

Retrying Sequences

Sometimes errors just happen and there's not much we can do about it. For example, there could be a timeout requesting remote data because the user has a spotty Internet connection, or a remote server we're querying could crash. In these cases it would be great if we could keep requesting the data we need until we succeed. The retry operator does exactly that:

```
ch2/6_error_handling.js
// This will try to retrieve the remote URL up to five times.
Observable.ajax("/products")
  .retry(5)
  .subscribe(
    xhr => console.log(xhr),
    err => console.error("ERROR: ", err)
  );
```

In the preceding code, we create a function that returns an Observable that retrieves contents from a URL. Because our connection might be a bit spotty, we add retry(5) before subscribing to it, ensuring that in case of an error, it will try up to five times before giving up and showing an error.

There are two important things to know when using retry. First, if we don't pass any parameters, it will retry indefinitely until the sequence is finished with no errors. This is dangerous for performance if the Observable keeps producing errors. If we're using synchronous Observables, it would have the same effect as an infinite loop.

Second, retry will always retry the whole Observable sequence again, even if some of the items didn't error. This is important in case you're causing any side effects when processing items, since they will be reapplied with every retry.

Making a Real-Time Earthquake Visualizer

Using the concepts that we've covered so far in this chapter, we'll build a web application that uses RxJS to show us where earthquakes are happening in real time. We'll start by building a functional but naive reactive implementation, and we'll improve it as we go. The final result will look like this:

Preparing Our Environment

We'll use the USGS (U.S. Geological Survey) earthquake database,[1] which offers a real-time earthquake dataset in several formats. We will get our data from the weekly dataset in JSONP format.

We'll also use Leaflet, a JavaScript library, to render interactive maps.[2] We can add it to our project using NPM:

```
$ npm install leaflet --save
```

Let's see how our initialization code looks, and go over the important points:

---

1. http://earthquake.usgs.gov/earthquakes/feed/v1.0/
2. http://leafletjs.com

ch2/earthquake-visualizer/src/index.js

```
import { Observable } from "rxjs";
import L from "leaflet";

const QUAKE_URL = `http://earthquake.usgs.gov/earthquakes/
feed/v1.0/summary/all_day.geojsonp`;
```

❶
```
function loadJSONP(url) {
  const script = document.createElement("script");
  script.type = "text/javascript";
  script.src = url;

  const head = document.getElementsByTagName("head")[0];
  head.appendChild(script);
}
```

❷
```
const mapContainer = document.createElement("div");
mapContainer.id = "map";
document.body.appendChild(mapContainer);
```

❸
```
const map = L.map("map").setView([33.858631, -118.279602], 7);
```
❹
```
L.tileLayer("http://{s}.tile.osm.org/{z}/{x}/{y}.png").addTo(map);
```

❶ That's a helper function we use to load JSONP content. It creates a script element with its URL property pointing to a particular JavaScript script. Once we append it to <head>, the contents of the script will be executed.

❷ This is the placeholder div element that Leaflet will use to render our map.

❸ We initialize the Leaflet map by setting the coordinates to the center of Los Angeles (plenty of earthquakes there!) with a reasonable zoom level.

❹ We tell Leaflet to set the default tile set for our map. The tile set is just a "theme" for our map.

Retrieving Earthquake Locations

Now that our initialization code is ready, we can write the logic for our application. First we need to know what kind of data we get and what data we need to represent earthquakes on a map.

The JSONP data that the USGS site gives us back looks like this:

```
eqfeed_callback({
  "type": "FeatureCollection",
  "metadata": {
    "generated": 1408030886000,
    "url": "http://earthquake.usgs.gov/earthquakes/...",
    "title": "USGS All Earthquakes, Past Day",
    "status": 200, "api": "1.0.13", "count": 134
  },
```

```
"features": [
  {
    "type": "Feature",
    "properties": {
      "mag": 0.82,
      "title": "M 0.8 - 3km WSW of Idyllwild-Pine Cove, California",
      "place": "3km WSW of Idyllwild-Pine Cove, California",
      "time": 1408030368460,
      ...
    },
    "geometry": {
      "type": "Point",
      "coordinates": [ -116.7636667, 33.7303333, 17.33 ]
    },
    "id": "ci15538377"
  },
  ...
]
})
```

The features array contains an object with the data for every earthquake that happened today. That's a truckload of data! It's amazing (and terrifying) how many earthquakes happen in a single day. For our program we'll need only the coordinates, title, and magnitude for each earthquake.

We first want to create an Observable that retrieves the dataset and emits single earthquakes. Here's a first version:

ch2/earthquake-visualizer/src/index.js
```
const quakes$ = Observable.create(observer => {
  window.eqfeed_callback = response => {
    response.features.forEach(observer.next);
  };

  loadJSONP(QUAKE_URL);
});

quakes$.subscribe(quake => {
  const coords = quake.geometry.coordinates;
  const size = quake.properties.mag * 10000;

  L.circle([coords[1], coords[0]], size).addTo(map);
});
```

Wait, what is that blatant global function window.eqfeed_callback doing in our code? It turns out that JSONP URLs often provide a way—by adding a query string in the URL—to specify the function name to handle the response, but the USGS site doesn't allow that, so we need to create a global function with the name they decided we must use, which is eqfeed_callback.

Joe asks:

What Is JSONP?

JSONP—or *JSON with padding*—is a sneaky technique that web developers came up with to work around the browser restrictions when requesting data from third-party domains.[a]

It bypasses these restrictions by loading external content using script tags instead of the usual XMLHttpRequest. Adding a script tag to the DOM loads and executes its content directly, and the security restrictions are not applied.

The remote request's content is then normal JSON wrapped in a function call (the *P* in JSONP). It looks like this:

```
callbackFn({ a: 1, b: 2, c: 3})
```

JSONP URLs usually accept a query string parameter so that the caller can specify the name of the callback. The developer then has to define a function in her code that has the same name as the callback in the server response, and when the script tag is added to the document, that function will be called with the JSON data as the first parameter.

Libraries like jQuery automate this process by internally creating the global function to handle the JSONP call, and tidying up afterward to avoid polluting the global namespace.

---

a.   http://en.wikipedia.org/wiki/Same-origin_policy

Our Observable emits all earthquakes in order. We have an earthquake generator now! We don't have to care about asynchronous flows or about having to put all of our logic in the same function. As long as we subscribe to the Observable, earthquakes will just come to us.

By having the earthquake retrieval "blackboxed" in the quakes$ Observable, we can now subscribe to it and process each earthquake. Then we'll draw a circle for each earthquake with a size proportional to its magnitude.

Going Deeper

Can we do better? You bet! In the preceding code, we're still managing flow by traversing the array and calling next to yield each earthquake, even if we isolated it inside the Observable. So much for reactiveness!

This is a perfect situation for flatMap. We'll retrieve the data and make an Observable out of the features array using Rx.Observable.from. Then we'll merge that Observable back in the main Observable. Here's how the quakes$ variable changes:

```
ch2/earthquake-visualizer/src/index.js
const quakes$ = Observable.create(observer => {
  window.eqfeed_callback = response => {
```
❶
```
    observer.next(response);
```
❷
```
    observer.complete();
  };

  loadJSONP(QUAKE_URL);
```
❸
```
}).flatMap(dataset => {
```
❹
```
  return Observable.from(dataset.features);
});
```

We're not manually managing the flow anymore. There are no loops or conditionals to extract the individual earthquake objects and pass them around. Here's what's happening:

❶ next only happens once, and it yields the whole JSON response.

❷ Since we'll yield only one time, we signal completion after next.

❸ We're chaining the flatMap call to the result of create, so flatMap will take each result from the Observable (in this case only one) and transform the Observable into one that yields every item of the dataset.features property by using Rx.Observable.from, which creates an Observable from any given iterable type, an array in our case.

❹ Here we take the features array containing all the earthquakes and create an Observable from it. Because of flatMap, this will become the actual Observable that the quakes$ variable will contain.

Creating Our Own loadJSONP

A good exercise at this point is to convert the helper loadJSONP function to Observable form, and make our flow completely stream-based. This implementation will be sightly more verbose than our previous simplistic function because it will add some functionality like error handling. Here it is:

```
ch2/earthquake-visualizer/src/index.js
function loadJSONP(settings) {
```
❶
```
  const url = settings.url;
  const callbackName = settings.callbackName;

  const script = document.createElement("script");
  script.type = "text/javascript";
  script.src = url;
```
❷
```
  window[callbackName] = data => {
    window[callbackName].data = data;
  };
```

```
❸     return Observable.create(observer => {
❹       const handler = e => {
          const status = e.type === "error" ? 400 : 200;
          const response = window[callbackName].data;

          if (status === 200) {
❺           observer.next({
              status,
              responseType: "jsonp",
              response,
              originalEvent: e
            });

            observer.complete();
          } else {
❻           observer.error({
              type: "error",
              status,
              originalEvent: e
            });
          }
        };

❼       script.onload = script.onreadystatechanged = script.onerror = handler;

        const head = window.document.getElementsByTagName("head")[0];
        head.insertBefore(script, head.firstChild);
      });
    }
```

❶ loadJSONP gets a settings parameter that contains the url and callbackName.

❷ Here we create a global function in the browser window object with the name of the JSONP callback. When the JSONP script is loaded, it will store the JSON in the data property of that function.

❸ Our Observable is quite specific, so we use the create operator to have total freedom to write our logic.

❹ The handler function receives an event as a parameter. This event is emitted when our JSONP script has been loaded (see below).

❺ If there are no errors loading the script, we call observer.next with an object that contains some metadata and a property response, which contains our JSON. After that, we call Rx.Observable.complete to signal that this observable yielded its one and only value and it's finished.

❻ If for any reason the remote JSONP script could not be loaded, we call Rx.Observable.error to signal an error in the sequence. We call error with an object that contains some useful metadata for debugging.

❼ Finally, we assign our handler function to event listeners that listen for remote script events like loading status and errors.

Making It Real Time

Our reactive version of the earthquake application doesn't update the map of earthquakes in real time. To implement that, we'll use the interval operator (which we saw earlier in this chapter) and the über-useful distinct operator. Let me show you the final code and then we'll go through the changes:

```
ch2/earthquake-visualizer/src/index.js
const quakes$ = Observable.interval(5000)
  .flatMap(() => {
    return loadJSONP({
      url: QUAKE_URL,
      callbackName: "eqfeed_callback"
    }).retry(3);
  })
  .flatMap(result => Observable.from(result.response.features))
  .distinct(quake => quake.properties.code);

quakes$.subscribe(quake => {
  const coords = quake.geometry.coordinates;
  const size = quake.properties.mag * 10000;

  L.circle([coords[1], coords[0]], size).addTo(map);
});
```

In the preceding code, we abuse interval to make new requests and process them at regular intervals of five seconds. interval creates an Observable that emits an incrementing number every five seconds. We don't do anything with those numbers; instead, we use flatMap to retrieve the data of the jsonpRequest. Notice also how we use retry to try again in case there are problems retrieving the list at first.

The last operator we apply is distinct, which emits only elements that haven't been emitted before. It takes a function that returns the property to check for equality. This way we never redraw earthquakes that are already drawn.

In less than 20 lines (without counting our loadJSONP implementation), we've written an application that regularly polls an external JSONP URL, extracts concrete data from its contents, and then filters out earthquakes that have already been imported. After that, we represent the earthquakes on a map, with a size proportional to their magnitude—all written in a self-contained, clear, and concise way, without relying on external state. Not bad at all! That shows how expressive Observables can be.

Ideas for Improvements

Here are a couple of ideas to put your newly acquired RxJS skills to use and make this little application a bit more interesting:

- When the user hovers the mouse over an earthquake, offer a pop-up that shows more information about that particular earthquake. One way to do that would be to create a new Observable from the quakes$ one with just the properties you want to show, and dynamically filter it upon hovering.

- Implement a counter at the top of the page that shows the number of earthquakes so far today and resets every day.

Operator Rundown

This chapter presented you with a few new operators, so here's a recap of them, along with some scenarios for ways we can use them in our applications (remember, you can always find the complete API documentation for operators on the RxJS GitHub site[3]):

- Rx.Observable.from

  Default behavior: *Synchronous*

  Since many of the data sources you use in your applications will come from arrays or iterables, it makes sense to have an operator that creates Observables out of them. from is one of the operators you'll use the most.

  With from we can create Observables from arrays, array-like objects (for instance, the arguments object or DOM NodeLists), and even types that implement the iterable protocol, such as String, Map, and Set.[4]

- Rx.Observable.range

  Default behavior: *Synchronous*

  The range operator generates finite Observables that emit integers in a particular range. It is extremely versatile and can be used in many scenarios. For example, you could use range to generate the initial squares on the board of a game like Minesweeper.

---

3. https://github.com/ReactiveX/rxjs/blob/master/doc/operators.md

4. https://developer.mozilla.org/ca/docs/Web/JavaScript/Reference/Iteration_protocols

- Rx.Observable.interval

  Default behavior: *Asynchronous*

  Each time you need to generate values spaced in time, you'll probably start with an interval operator as the generator. Since interval emits sequential integers every x milliseconds (where *x* is a parameter we pass), we just need to transform the values to whatever we want. Our game in Chapter 3, *Building Concurrent Programs*, on page 39, is heavily based on that technique.

- Rx.Observable.distinct

  Default behavior: *Same as the Observable it filters*

  distinct is one of these simple operators that saves a ton of work. It filters out of the sequence any value that has already been emitted. That keeps us from writing time and again that error-prone boilerplate code that uses a dictionary somewhere with the emitted results, against which we compare incoming results. You know what kind of code I'm talking about. Yuck. That's gone with distinct.

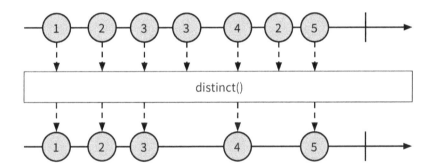

  distinct lets us use a function that specifies the comparison method. Additionally, we can pass no arguments and it will use strict comparison to compare primitives such as numbers or strings, and run deep comparisons in case of more complex objects.

Wrapping Up

In this chapter we covered how to visually represent and understand Observable flows using marble diagrams. We've covered the most common operators to transform Observables, and, more importantly, we've built a real-world application using only Observable sequences, avoiding setting any external state, loops, or conditional branches. We expressed our whole program in a declarative way, without having to encode every step to accomplish the task at hand.

In the next chapter we'll continue to explore Observable sequences, this time taking a look at more advanced operators that allow you to control and bend flows and data in your program like you've never imagined possible with procedural code!

CHAPTER 3

Building Concurrent Programs

Concurrency is the art of doing several things at the same time, correctly and efficiently. To accomplish this, we structure our programs to take advantage of time so that tasks run together in the most efficient way. Examples of everyday concurrency in applications include keeping the user interface responsive while other activities are happening, and processing hundreds of customers' orders effectively.

In this chapter we'll explore concurrency and pure functions in RxJS by making a shoot-'em-up spaceship game for the browser. We'll first introduce the Observable pipeline, a technique to chain Observable operators and pass state between them. Then I'll show you how to use the pipeline to build programs without relying on external state or side effects, by encapsulating all your logic and state inside the Observables themselves.

Video games are computer programs that need to keep a lot of state, but we'll write our game with no external state whatsoever, using the power of the Observable pipeline and some great RxJS operators.

Purity and the Observable Pipeline

An Observable pipeline is a group of operators chained together, where each one takes an Observable as input and returns an Observable as output. We've been using pipelines in this book; they are ubiquitous when programming with RxJS. Here's a simple one:

```
ch3/pipeline.js
Observable
  .from([1, 2, 3, 4, 5, 6, 7, 8])
  .filter(val => val % 2)
  .map(val => val * 10);
```

Pipelines are self-contained. All state flows from one operator to the next without the need for any external variables. This way we avoid external state (we talked about external state in *Side Effects and External State*, on page 5). We accomplish this by using pure functions.

Pure functions always return the same output given the same input. It's easier to design programs with high concurrency when we can guarantee that a function in the program can't modify state other functions rely on.

Avoiding External State

In the following example we count the even numbers that interval has yielded so far. We do that by creating an Observable from interval ticks and increasing evenTicks when the tick we receive is an even number:

```
ch3/state.js
let evenTicks = 0;

function updateDistance(i) {
  if (i % 2 === 0) {
    evenTicks += 1;
  }
  return evenTicks;
}
const ticksObservable = Observable.interval(1000).map(updateDistance);

ticksObservable.subscribe(() => {
  console.log(`Subscriber 1 - evenTicks: ${evenTicks} so far`);
});
```

This is the output we get after the program has been running for four seconds:

```
‹  Subscriber 1 - evenTicks: 1 so far
   Subscriber 1 - evenTicks: 1 so far
   Subscriber 1 - evenTicks: 2 so far
   Subscriber 1 - evenTicks: 2 so far
```

Now, just for kicks, let's add another subscriber to ticksObservable:

```
ch3/state.js
let evenTicks = 0;

function updateDistance(i) {
  if (i % 2 === 0) {
    evenTicks += 1;
  }
  return evenTicks;
}
```

```
const ticksObservable = Observable.interval(1000).map(updateDistance);

ticksObservable.subscribe(() => {
  console.log(`Subscriber 1 - evenTicks: ${evenTicks} so far`);
});

ticksObservable.subscribe(() => {
  console.log(`Subscriber 2 - evenTicks: ${evenTicks} so far`);
});
```

The output is now the following:

```
Subscriber 1 - evenTicks: 1 so far
Subscriber 2 - evenTicks: 2 so far
Subscriber 1 - evenTicks: 2 so far
Subscriber 2 - evenTicks: 2 so far
Subscriber 1 - evenTicks: 3 so far
Subscriber 2 - evenTicks: 4 so far
Subscriber 1 - evenTicks: 4 so far
Subscriber 2 - evenTicks: 4 so far
```

Hold on a second—the evenTicks count on Subscriber 2 is completely off! It should always contain the same evenTicks count as Subscriber 1. The reason, as you might have guessed, is that the Observable pipeline will run once for each subscriber, increasing evenTicks twice.

Problems caused by sharing external state are often more subtle than this example. In complex applications, opening the door to changing state outside of the pipeline leads to code becoming complicated, and bugs soon start to show up. The solution is to encapsulate as much information as we can inside the pipeline. Here's a way we could refactor the preceding code to avoid external state:

ch3/state.js
```
function updateDistance(acc, i) {
  if (i % 2 === 0) {
    acc += 1;
  }
  return acc;
}

const ticksObservable = Observable.interval(1000).scan(updateDistance, 0);

ticksObservable.subscribe(evenTicks => {
  console.log(`Subscriber 1 - evenTicks: ${evenTicks} so far`);
});

ticksObservable.subscribe(evenTicks => {
  console.log(`Subscriber 2 - evenTicks: ${evenTicks} so far`);
});
```

And the expected output:

```
Subscriber 1 - evenTicks: 1 so far
Subscriber 2 - evenTicks: 1 so far
Subscriber 1 - evenTicks: 1 so far
Subscriber 2 - evenTicks: 1 so far
Subscriber 1 - evenTicks: 2 so far
Subscriber 2 - evenTicks: 2 so far
Subscriber 1 - evenTicks: 2 so far
Subscriber 2 - evenTicks: 2 so far
```

Using scan, we avoid external state altogether. We pass the accumulated count of even ticks to updateDistance instead of relying on an external variable to keep the accumulated value.

Most of the time we can avoid relying on external state. Common scenarios for using it are caching values or keeping track of changing values in the program. But, as you'll see in *Spaceship Reactive!*, on page 50, these scenarios can be handled in several other ways. For example, when we need to cache values, *RxJS's Subject Class*, on page 44, can help a lot, and when we need to keep track of previous states of the game, we can use methods like Rx.Observable.scan.

Pipelines Are Efficient

The first time I chained a bunch of operators into a pipeline to transform a sequence, my gut feeling was that it couldn't possibly be efficient. I knew transforming arrays in JavaScript by chaining operators is expensive. Yet in this book I'm telling you to design your program by transforming sequences into new ones. Isn't that terribly inefficient?

Chaining looks similar in Observables and in arrays; there are even methods like filter and map that are present in both types. But there's a crucial difference: array methods create a new array as a result of each operation, which is traversed entirely by the next operation. Observable pipelines, on the other hand, don't create intermediate Observables and apply all operations to each element in one go. The Observable is thus traversed only once, which makes chaining Observables efficient. Check out the following example:

```
ch3/array_chain.js
stringArray // Represents an array of 1,000 strings
❶  .map(str => str.toUpperCase())
❷  .filter(/^[A-Z]+$/.test)
❸  .forEach(str => console.log(str));
```

Let's suppose stringArray is an array with 1,000 strings that we want to convert to uppercase and then filter out the ones that contain anything other than alphabet characters (or no letters at all). Then we want to print each string of the resulting array to the console.

This is what happens behind the scenes:

❶ Iterate through the array and create a new array with all items uppercase.

❷ Iterate through the uppercase array, creating another array with 1,000 elements.

❸ Iterate through the filtered array and log each result to the console.

In the process of transforming the array, we've iterated arrays three times and created two completely new big arrays. This is far from efficient! You shouldn't program this way if you're concerned about performance or you're dealing with big sequences of items.

This is what the same operation would look like using Observables:

ch3/array_chain.js
```
stringObservable$ // Represents an observable emitting 1,000 strings
   .map(str => str.toUpperCase())
   .filter(/^[A-Z]+$/.test)
   .subscribe(str => console.log(str));
```

Observable pipelines look extremely similar to array chains, but their similarities end here. In an Observable, nothing ever happens until we subscribe to it, no matter how many queries and transformations we apply to it. When we chain a transformation like map, we're composing a single function that will operate on every item of the array once. So, in the preceding code, this is what will happen:

❶ Create an uppercase function that will be applied to each item of the Observable and return an Observable that will emit these new items, whenever an Observer subscribes to it.

❷ Compose a filter function with the previous uppercase function, and return an Observable that will emit the new items, uppercased and filtered, but only when we subscribe to it.

❸ Trigger the Observable to emit items, going through all of them only once and applying the transformations we defined once per item.

With Observables, we'll go through our list only once, and we'll apply the transformations only if absolutely required. For example, let's say we added a take operator to our previous example:

ch3/array_chain.js
```
stringObservable$
  .map(str => str.toUpperCase())
  .filter(/^[A-Z]+$/.test)
  .take(5)
  .subscribe(str => console.log(str));
```

take makes the Observable emit only the first n items we specify. In our case, n is five, so out of the thousand strings, we'll receive only the first five. The cool part is that our code will never traverse all the items; it will apply our transformations to only the first five.

This makes the developer's life much easier. You can rest assured that when manipulating sequences, RxJS will do only as much work as necessary. This way of operating is called *lazy evaluation*, and it is very common in functional languages such as Haskell and Miranda.

RxJS's Subject Class

A Subject is a type that implements both Observer and Observable types. As an Observer, it can subscribe to Observables, and as an Observable it can produce values and have Observers subscribe to it.

In some scenarios a single Subject can do the work of a combination of Observers and Observables. For example, for making a proxy object between a data source and the Subject's listeners, we could use this:

ch3/subjects.js
```
import { Subject, Observable } from 'rxjs/Observable';

const subject$ = new Subject();
const source$ = Observable
.interval(300)
.map(v => `Interval message #${v}`)
.take(5);

source$.subscribe(subject$);

subject$.subscribe(
  next => console.log(`Next: ${next}`),
  error => console.log(`Error: ${error.message}`),
  () => console.log('Completed!')
);

subject$.next('Our message #1');
subject$.next('Our message #2');

setTimeout(subject$.complete, 1000);
```

Output:

```
onNext: Our message #1
onNext: Our message #2
onNext: Interval message #0
onNext: Interval message #1
onNext: Interval message #2
onCompleted
```

In the preceding example we create a new Subject and a source Observable that emits an integer every 300 milliseconds. Then we subscribe the Subject to the Observable. After that, we subscribe an Observer to the Subject itself. The Subject now behaves as an Observable.

Next we make the Subject emit values of its own (message1 and message2). In the final result, we get the Subject's own messages and then the proxied values from the source Observable. The values from the Observable come later because they are asynchronous, whereas we made the Subject's own values immediate. Notice that even if we tell the source Observable to take the first five values, the output shows only the first three. That's because after one second we call onCompleted on the Subject. This finishes the notifications to all subscriptions and overrides the take operator in this case.

The Subject class provides the base for creating more specialized Subjects. In fact, RxJS comes with some interesting ones: AsyncSubject, BehaviorSubject, and ReplaySubject.

AsyncSubject

AsyncSubject emits the last value of a sequence only if the sequence completes. This value is then cached forever, and any Observer that subscribes after the value has been emitted will receive it right away. AsyncSubject is convenient for asynchronous operations that return a single value, such as Ajax requests.

Let's see a simple example of an AsyncSubject subscribing to a range:

```
ch3/subjects.js
import { AsyncSubject, Observable } from 'rxjs/Observable';

const delayedRange$ = Observable.range(0, 5).delay(1000);
const subject$ = new AsyncSubject();

delayedRange$.subscribe(subject$);

subject$.subscribe(
  next => console.log('Value:', next),
  error => console.log('Error:', error),
  () => console.log('Completed.')
);
```

In that example, delayedRange emits the values 0 to 4 after a delay of a second. Then we create a new AsyncSubject subject and subscribe it to delayedRange. The output is the following:

```
Value: 4
Completed.
```

As expected, we get only the last value that the Observer emits. Let's now use AsyncSubject for a more realistic scenario. We'll retrieve some remote content:

```
ch3/subjects.js
import { AsyncSubject, Observable } from 'rxjs/Observable';

function getProducts(url) {
  let subject$;

  return Observable.create(observer$ => {

    if (!subject$) {
      subject$ = new AsyncSubject();
      Observable.ajax(url).subscribe(subject$);
    }
    return subject$.subscribe(observer$);
  });
}

const products$ = getProducts('/products');
// Will trigger request and receive the response when read
products$
  .subscribe(
    next => console.log('Result 1:', next.response),
    error => console.log('ERROR', error)
  );

// Will receive the result immediately because it's cached
setTimeout(
  () => {

    products$.subscribe(
      next => console.log('Result 2:', next.response),
      error => console.log('ERROR', error)
    );
  },
  5000
);
```

In this code, when getProducts is called with a URL, it returns an Observer that emits the result of the HTTP GET request. Here's how it breaks down:

❶ getProducts returns an Observable sequence. We create it here.

❷ If we haven't created an AsyncSubject yet, we create it and subscribe it to the Observable that Rx.DOM.Request.get(url) returns.

❸ We subscribe the Observer to the AsyncSubject. Every time an Observer subscribes to the Observable, it will actually be subscribed to the AsyncSubject, which is acting as a proxy between the Observable retrieving the URL and the Observers.

❹ We create the Observable that retrieves the URL "products" and store it in the products variable.

❺ This is the first subscription and will kick off the URL retrieval and log the results when the URL is retrieved.

❻ This is the second subscription, which runs five seconds after the first one. Since at that time the URL has already been retrieved, there's no need for another network request. It will receive the result of the request immediately because it is already stored in the AsyncSubject subject.

The interesting bit is that we're using an AsyncSubject that subscribes to the Rx.DOM.Request.get Observable. Because AsyncSubject caches the last result, any subsequent subscription to products will receive the result right away, without causing another network request. We can use AsyncSubject whenever we expect a single result and want to hold onto it.

BehaviorSubject

When an Observer subscribes to a BehaviorSubject, it receives the last emitted value and then all the subsequent values. BehaviorSubject requires that we provide a starting value, so that all Observers will always receive a value when they subscribe to a BehaviorSubject. Imagine we want to retrieve a remote file and print its contents on an HTML page, but we want placeholder text while we wait for the contents. We can use a BehaviorSubject for this:

```
ch3/behavior_subject.js
import { Observable, BehaviorSubject } from "rxjs";

const subject$ = new BehaviorSubject('Waiting for content');

subject$.subscribe(
  next => {
    document.body.textContent = next.response || next;
  },
  error => {
    document.body.textContent = 'There was an error retrieving content';
  }
);

Observable.ajax('/remote/content').subscribe(subject$);
```

In the code, we initialize a new BehaviorSubject with our placeholder content. Then we subscribe to it and change the HTML body content in both onNext and onError, depending on the result.

Now the HTML body contains our placeholder text, and it will stay that way until the Subject emits a new value. Finally, we request the resource we want and we subscribe our Subject to the resulting Observer.

BehaviorSubject guarantees that there will always be at least one value emitted, because we provide a default value in its constructor. Once the BehaviorSubject completes it won't emit any more values, freeing the memory used by the cached value.

ReplaySubject

A ReplaySubject caches its values and re-emits them to any Observer that subscribes late to it. Unlike with AsyncSubject, the sequence doesn't need to be completed for this to happen.

Subject	ReplaySubject
`const subject$ = new Rx.Subject();`	`const subject$ = new Rx.ReplaySubject();`
`subject$.next(1);`	`subject$.next(1);`

`subject$.subscribe(n => {`
`  console.log('Received value:', n);`
`});`
	`subject$.subscribe(n => {`
	`  console.log('Received value:', n);`
	`});`

`subject$.next(2);` `subject$.next(3);`	`subject$.next(2);` `subject$.next(3);`
‹ Received value: 2 Received value: 3	‹ Received value: 1 Received value: 2 Received value: 3

ReplaySubject is useful to make sure that Observers get all the values emitted by an Observable from the start. It spares us from writing messy code that caches previous values, saving us from nasty concurrency-related bugs.

Of course, to accomplish that behavior ReplaySubject caches all values in memory. To prevent it from using too much memory, we can limit the amount of data it stores by buffer size or window of time, or by passing particular parameters to the constructor.

The first parameter to the constructor of ReplaySubject takes a number that represents how many values we want to buffer:

> ⦚⦚
> ⦚
>
> **Joe asks:**
>
> # Does That Mean
> # AsyncSubject Acts Like a Promise?
>
> Indeed.
>
> AsyncSubject represents the result of an asynchronous action, and you can use it as a substitute for a promise. The difference internally is that a promise will only ever process a single value, whereas AsyncSubject processes all values in a sequence, only ever emitting (and caching) the last one.
>
> Being able to so easily simulate promises shows the flexibility of the RxJS model. (Even without AsyncSubject, it would be pretty easy to simulate a promise using Observables.)

```
const subject$ = new Rx.ReplaySubject(2); // Buffer size of 2

subject$.next(1);
subject$.next(2);
subject$.next(3);

subject$.subscribe(n => {
  console.log('Received value:', n);
});
```

❮ Received value: 2
Received value: 3

The second parameter takes a number that represents the time in milliseconds during which we want to buffer values:

```
const subject$ = new Rx.ReplaySubject(null, 200); // Buffer size of 200ms

setTimeout(() => subject$.next(1), 100);
setTimeout(() => subject$.next(2), 200);
setTimeout(() => subject$.next(3), 300);
setTimeout(
  () => {
    subject$.subscribe(n => {
      console.log('Received value:', n);
    });

    subject$.next(4);
  },
  350
);
```

In this example we set a buffer based on time, instead of the number of values. Our ReplaySubject will cache values that were emitted up to 200 milliseconds ago. We emit three values, each separated by 100 milliseconds, and after 350 milliseconds we subscribe an Observer and we emit yet another value. At the moment of the subscription the items cached are *2* and *3*, because *1* happened too long ago (around 250 milliseconds ago), so it is no longer cached.

Subjects are a powerful tool that can save you a lot of time. They provide great solutions to common scenarios like caching and repeating. And since at their core they are just Observables and Observers, you don't need to learn anything new.

Spaceship Reactive!

To show how we can keep an application pure, we'll build a video game in which our hero fights endless hordes of enemy spaceships. We'll make heavy use of Observable pipelines, and I'll point out along the way when it might be tempting to store state outside the pipeline and how to avoid it.

Video games notoriously keep a lot of external state—scores, screen coordinates for the characters, timers, and so on. Our plan is to build the whole game without relying on a single external variable that keeps state.

In our game, the player will move the spaceship horizontally using the mouse, and will shoot by clicking the mouse or tapping the spacebar. It will have four main actors: the moving star field in the background, the player's spaceship, the enemies, and the shots from both the player and the enemies.

It will look like this:

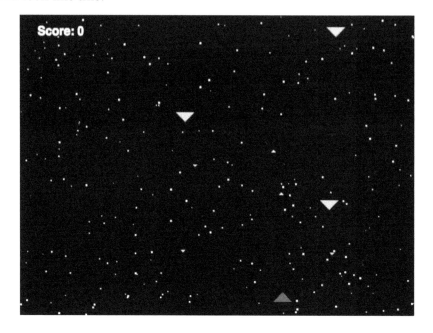

In the screenshot, the red triangle is our spaceship and the green ones are the enemies. The tiny, yellow triangles are the fired shots.

Let's start by setting the stage; this will be our HTML file:

```
ch3/spaceship.html
<!DOCTYPE html>
<html>
  <head>
    <meta charset="utf-8">
    <title>Spaceship Reactive!</title>
    <script src="https://unpkg.com/rxjs@5.5.0/bundles/Rx.min.js"></script>
    <style>
      html, body {
        margin: 0;
        padding: 0;
      }
    </style>
  </head>
  <body>
    <script src="spaceship.js"></script>
  </body>
</html>
```

It's just a simple HTML file that loads the JavaScript file we'll be working with for the rest of the chapter. In that JavaScript file, we start by setting up a canvas element where we'll render our game:

```
const canvas = document.createElement('canvas');
const ctx = canvas.getContext('2d');
document.body.appendChild(canvas);
canvas.width = window.innerWidth;
canvas.height = window.innerHeight;
```

With this in place we can start describing our game's components. First let's draw our starry background.

Creating the Star Field

Our game is set in space, so we need stars: lots of them! We'll create a star field that scrolls down to give the feeling of traveling through space. For this, we'll first generate the stars using the range operator:

```
ch3/starfield_1.js
const SPEED = 40;
const STAR_NUMBER = 250;
const StarStream$ = Observable
```

```
.range(1, STAR_NUMBER)
.map(() => ({
  x: parseInt(Math.random() * canvas.width, 10),
  y: parseInt(Math.random() * canvas.height, 10),
  size: Math.random() * 3 + 1
}))
```

Each star will be represented by an object that contains random coordinates and a size between 1 and 4. This code will give us a stream that generates 250 "stars."

We want these stars to keep moving. A way to do that is to increase the y-coordinate every few milliseconds for all stars. We'll transform the StarStream Observable into a single array using toArray, which will contain all the star objects. Then we can use flatMap to transform the Observable into a timer that emits every few milliseconds using interval. Every time the interval emits, we'll increase the y-coordinate in each star in the original array. We can even get a nice parallax effect for free by moving each star a distance the same as its size:

ch3/starfield_1.js
```
const SPEED = 40;
const STAR_NUMBER = 250;
const StarStream$ = Observable
  .range(1, STAR_NUMBER)
  .map(() => ({
    x: parseInt(Math.random() * canvas.width, 10),
    y: parseInt(Math.random() * canvas.height, 10),
    size: Math.random() * 3 + 1
  }))
  .toArray()
  .flatMap(starArray => Observable.interval(SPEED).map(() => {
    starArray.forEach(star => {
      if (star.y >= canvas.height) {
        star.y = 0; // Reset star to top of the screen
      }
      star.y += star.size; // Move star
    });

    return starArray;
  }))
```

Inside map we check if the star y-coordinate is already outside the screen, and in this case we reset it to 0. By changing the coordinates in every star object we can keep using the same array of stars all the time.

Now we need a helper function that "paints" an array of stars on our canvas:

ch3/starfield_1.js
```
function paintStars(stars) {
  ctx.fillStyle = '#000000';
  ctx.fillRect(0, 0, canvas.width, canvas.height);
  ctx.fillStyle = '#ffffff';
  stars.forEach(star => {
    ctx.fillRect(star.x, star.y, star.size, star.size);
  });
}
```

paintStars paints a black background and draws the stars on the canvas. The only thing left to achieve a moving star field is to subscribe to the Observable and call paintStars with the resulting array. Here's the final code:

ch3/starfield_1.js
```
function paintStars(stars) {
  ctx.fillStyle = '#000000';
  ctx.fillRect(0, 0, canvas.width, canvas.height);
  ctx.fillStyle = '#ffffff';
  stars.forEach(star => {
    ctx.fillRect(star.x, star.y, star.size, star.size);
  });
}

const SPEED = 40;
const STAR_NUMBER = 250;
const StarStream$ = Observable
  .range(1, STAR_NUMBER)
  .map(() => ({
    x: parseInt(Math.random() * canvas.width, 10),
    y: parseInt(Math.random() * canvas.height, 10),
    size: Math.random() * 3 + 1
  }))
  .toArray()
  .flatMap(starArray => Observable.interval(SPEED).map(() => {
    starArray.forEach(star => {
      if (star.y >= canvas.height) {
        star.y = 0; // Reset star to top of the screen
      }
      star.y += star.size; // Move star
    });

    return starArray;
  }))
  .subscribe(paintStars);
```

The stage is set; it's time for our hero to make an appearance.

Adding the Player's Spaceship

Now that we have our beautiful starry background, we're ready to program the hero's spaceship. Even though it's the most important object in the game, our spaceship is deceptively simple. It's an Observer of mouse moves that emits the current mouse x-coordinate and a constant y-coordinate (the player only moves horizontally, so we never change the y-coordinate):

ch3/hero_1.js
```js
const HERO_Y = canvas.height - 30;
const mouseMove = Observable.fromEvent(canvas, 'mousemove');
const SpaceShip = mouseMove
  .map(event => ({
    x: event.clientX,
    y: HERO_Y
  }))
  .startWith({
    x: canvas.width / 2,
    y: HERO_Y
  });
```

Notice that I used startWith(). This sets the first value in the Observable, and I set it to a position in the middle of the screen. Without startWith our Observable would start emitting only when the player moves the mouse.

Let's render our hero on the screen. In this game all the characters are triangles (that's all my graphic-design skills can manage), so we'll define a helper function to render triangles on the canvas, given the coordinates, size, and color, and the direction they're facing:

ch3/hero_1.js
```js
function drawTriangle(x, y, width, color, direction) {
  ctx.fillStyle = color;
  ctx.beginPath();
  ctx.moveTo(x - width, y);
  ctx.lineTo(x, direction === 'up' ? y - width : y + width);
  ctx.lineTo(x + width, y);
  ctx.lineTo(x - width, y);
  ctx.fill();
}
```

We'll also define paintSpaceShip, which uses the helper function:

ch3/hero_1.js
```js
function paintSpaceShip(x, y) {
  drawTriangle(x, y, 20, '#ff0000', 'up');
}
```

But we're facing a problem now. If we subscribe to the SpaceShip Observable and call drawTriangle in the subscription, our spaceship would be visible only when we move the mouse, and for just an instant. This is because starStream is updating the canvas many times per second, erasing our spaceship if we don't move the mouse. And because the starStream doesn't have direct access to the spaceship, we can't render the spaceship in the starStream subscription. We could save the latest spaceship coordinates to a variable that the starStream can access, but then we would be breaking our rule of not modifying external state. What to do?

As is usually the case, RxJS has a very convenient operator we can use to solve our problem.

Rx.Observable.combineLatest is a handy operator. It takes two or more Observables and emits the last result of each Observable whenever any of them emits a new value. Knowing that starStream emits a new item (the array of stars) so frequently, we can remove the starStream subscription and use combineLatest to combine both the starStream and SpaceShip Observables and update them as soon as any of them emits a new item:

```
ch3/hero_1.js
function renderScene(actors) {
  paintStars(actors.stars);
  paintSpaceShip(actors.spaceship.x, actors.spaceship.y);
}

const Game = Observable.combineLatest(StarStream, SpaceShip, (
  stars,
  spaceship
) => ({
  stars,
  spaceship
}));

Game.subscribe(renderScene);
```

We're now using a function renderScene to paint everything on the screen, so you can remove the following subscription code for StarStream:

```
.subscribe(function(starArray) {
    paintStars(starArray);
});
```

With this, we'll paint the starry background *and* the spaceship every time any Observable emits a new item. We now have a spaceship flying through space, and we can move it at will using our mouse. Not bad for so little code! But our hero's spaceship is too lonely in the vastness of space. What about giving it some company?

Generating Enemies

It would be a very boring game if we didn't have any enemies to gun down. So let's create an infinite stream of them! We want to create a new enemy every second and a half to not overwhelm our hero. Let's look at the code for the Enemies Observable and then go through it:

```
ch3/enemy_1.js
const ENEMY_FREQ = 1500;
const Enemies = Observable.interval(ENEMY_FREQ).scan(enemyArray => {
  const enemy = {
    x: parseInt(Math.random() * canvas.width, 10),
    y: -30
  };

  enemyArray.push(enemy);
  return enemyArray;
}, []);

const Game = Observable.combineLatest(
  StarStream,
  SpaceShip,
  Enemies,
  (stars, spaceship, enemies) => ({
    stars,
    spaceship,
    enemies
  })
);

Game.subscribe(renderScene);
```

To create enemies, we use an interval operator to run every 1,500 milliseconds, and then we use the scan operator to create an array of enemies.

We briefly saw the scan operator in *Can We Aggregate Infinite Observables?*, on page 23. scan aggregates results each time an Observable emits a value, and emits each intermediate result. In the Enemies Observable we start with an empty array as scan's first parameter and we push a new object to it in every iteration. The object contains a random x-coordinate, and a fixed y-coordinate outside the visible screen. With this, Enemies will emit an array with all the current enemies every 1,500 milliseconds.

The only thing left to render enemies is a helper function to paint each of them on the canvas. This function will also be the one updating the coordinates of each item in the enemies array:

ch3/enemy_1.js

```
// Helper function to get a random integer
function getRandomInt(min, max) {
  return Math.floor(Math.random() * (max - min + 1)) + min;
}

function paintEnemies(enemies) {
  enemies.forEach(enemy => {
    enemy.y += 5;
    enemy.x += getRandomInt(-15, 15);

    drawTriangle(enemy.x, enemy.y, 20, "#00ff00", "down");
  });
}
```

You can see in paintEnemies that we are also changing the x-coordinate randomly so that enemies move a bit unpredictably to the sides. Now we need to update the function renderScene to include a call to paintEnemies.

You might have noticed a strange effect while playing the game we have so far: if you move the mouse, the enemies go faster toward you! That *could* be a nice feature in the game, but we definitely didn't intend to do that. Can you guess what causes this bug?

If you guessed that it was related to the paintEnemies function, you're right on the money. combineLatest renders our scene whenever any of the Observables yields a value. If we don't move the mouse, the fastest emitter will always be starStream because it has an interval of 40 milliseconds (the Enemies Observable emits only every 1,500 milliseconds). When we move the mouse, though, SpaceShip will emit faster than starStream (your mouse emits coordinates *many* times per second), and paintEnemies will then execute that many times, increasing the enemies' coordinates much faster.

To avoid this scenario and similar problems in the future, we need to normalize the game's speed so that no Observable can emit values faster than our chosen speed for the game.

And yes, as you may have guessed, RxJS has an operator for that.

Avoid Drinking from the Firehose

There is such a thing as receiving data too fast. Most of the time we want all the speed we can get, but depending on the frequency at which the Observable streams values, we might want to drop some of the values we receive. We're now in one of these scenarios. The speed at which we render things onscreen is proportional to the speed of the fastest Observable we have. It turns out that our fastest Observable is too fast for us, and we need to establish a constant update speed in the game.

sample is a method in Observable instances that, given a time parameter in milliseconds, returns an Observable that emits the last value emitted by the parent Observable in each time interval.

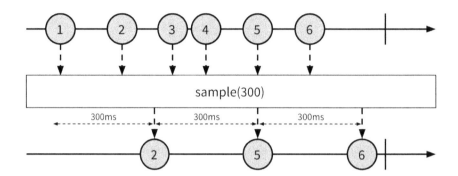

Notice how sample drops any values before the last value at the moment of the interval. It's important to consider whether you want this behavior. In our case, we don't care about dropping values because we just want to render the current state of each element every 40 milliseconds. If all the values are important to you, you might want to consider the buffer operator:

```
ch3/enemy_2.js
Observable
  .combineLatest(StarStream, SpaceShip, Enemies, (
    stars,
    spaceship,
    enemies
  ) => ({ stars, spaceship, enemies }))
  .sampleTime(SPEED)
  .subscribe(renderScene);
```

By calling sample after combineLatest we make sure that combineLatest will never yield any value faster than 40 milliseconds after the previous one (our constant SPEED is set to 40).

Shooting

It's a bit scary seeing the hordes of enemies coming at us; all we can do about it is move out of the way and hope they don't see us. How about we give our hero the ability to shoot at the evil alien spaceships?

We want our spaceship to shoot whenever we click the mouse or press the spacebar, so we'll create an Observable for each event and merge them into a single Observable called playerShots. Notice that we filter the *keydown* Observable by the key code of the spacebar, 32:

ch3/hero_shots.js
```
const playerFiring = Observable
  .merge(
    Observable.fromEvent(canvas, 'click'),
    Observable
      .fromEvent(document, 'keydown')
      .filter(evt => evt.keycode === 32)
  )
```

Now that we know about sample, we can use it to spice up the game and limit the shooting frequency of our spaceship. Otherwise, the player could shoot at high speed and destroy all enemies too easily. We'll make it so that the player can shoot only every 200 milliseconds at most:

ch3/hero_shots.js
```
const playerFiring = Observable
  .merge(
    Observable.fromEvent(canvas, 'click'),
    Observable
      .fromEvent(document, 'keydown')
      .filter(evt => evt.keycode === 32)
  )
  .startWith({})
  .sampleTime(200)
  .timestamp();
```

We've also added a timestamp operator, which sets a property *timestamp* in every value our Observable emits, with the exact time it is emitted. We'll use it later. Also, we use startWith to start with an initial shot so that we have an initial shot value for when we combine shots with the spaceship's position below.

Finally, to fire shots from our spaceship we need to know the x-coordinate of the spaceship at the firing moment. This is so we can render the shot at the correct x-coordinate. It may be tempting to set an external variable from the SpaceShip Observable that always contains the last x-coordinate emitted, but that would be breaking our unwritten agreement to never mutate external state!

Instead we'll accomplish this by using our good friend combineLatest again:

ch3/hero_shots.js
```js
const HeroShots = Observable
  .combineLatest(playerFiring, SpaceShip, (
    shotEvents,
    spaceShip
  ) => ({
    x: spaceShip.x
  }))
  .scan(
    (shotArray, shot) => {
      shotArray.push({
        x: shot.x,
        y: HERO_Y
      });
      return shotArray;
    },
    []
  );
```

We now get the updated values from SpaceShip and playerFiring, so we can get the x-coordinate we want. We use scan in the same way we used it for our Enemy Observable, creating an array of current coordinates for each of our shots. With that we should be ready to draw our shots on the screen. We use a helper function to draw every shot in the array of shots:

ch3/hero_shots.js
```js
const SHOOTING_SPEED = 15;
function paintHeroShots(heroShots) {
  heroShots.forEach(shot => {
    shot.y -= SHOOTING_SPEED;
    drawTriangle(shot.x, shot.y, 5, '#ffff00', 'up');
  });
}
```

Then we call paintHeroShots from our main combineLatest operation:

```js
Observable
  .combineLatest(StarStream, SpaceShip, Enemies, HeroShots, (
    stars,
    spaceship,
    enemies,
    heroShots
  ) => ({
    stars,
    spaceship,
    enemies,

    heroShots
  }))
  .sampleTime(SPEED)
  .subscribe(renderScene);
```

And we add a call to paintHeroShots inside renderScene:

```
function renderScene(actors) {
  paintStars(actors.stars);
  paintSpaceShip(actors.spaceship.x, actors.spaceship.y);
  paintEnemies(actors.enemies);
  paintHeroShots(actors.heroShots);
}
```

Now when you run the game you'll notice that *every* time you move the mouse, our spaceship fires an insane number of shots. Not bad for a visual effect, but that's not what we wanted! Let's look at the HeroShots Observable again. In it, we're using combineLatest so that we have values from playerFiring and SpaceShip. This looks similar to the problem we had before. combineLatest in HeroShots is emitting values every time the mouse moves, and this translates into shots being fired. Throttling won't help in this case, because we want the user to shoot whenever she wants, and throttling would limit the number of shots and drop many of them.

combineLatest emits the last value that each Observable emitted, whenever an Observable emits a new value. We can use this to our advantage. Whenever the mouse moves, combineLatest emits the new SpaceShip position and the last emitted value of playerFiring, which will be unchanged unless we fire a new shot. We can then emit a value *only* when the emitted shot is different from the previous one. The distinctUntilChanged operator does the dirty work for us as shown in the figures on page 62.

The operators distinct and distinctUntilChanged allow us to filter out results that an Observable has already emitted. distinct filters out any result previously emitted and distinctUntilChanged filters out identical results unless a different one is emitted in between. We only need to make sure that the new shot is different from the previous one, so distinctUntilChanged is enough for us. (It also saves us from the higher memory usage of distinct; distinct needs to keep all the previous results in memory.)

We modify heroShots so it only emits new shots, based on their timestamp:

```
ch3/hero_shots2.js
const HeroShots = Observable
  .combineLatest(playerFiring, SpaceShip, (
    shotEvents,
    spaceShip
  ) => ({
    timestamp: shotEvents.timestamp,
    x: spaceShip.x
  }))
```

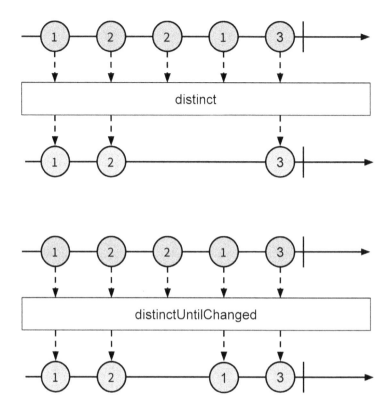

```
.distinctUntilChanged(shot => shot.timestamp)
.scan(
  (shotArray, shot) => {
    shotArray.push({
      x: shot.x,
      y: HERO_Y
    });
    return shotArray;
  },
  []
);
```

If everything went well, we're now able to shoot at enemies from our spaceship!

Enemy Shots

We should allow enemies to shoot as well; otherwise it's a pretty unfair universe. And a boring one! For enemy shots, we'll do the following:

- Each enemy will keep an updated array of its own shots.
- Each enemy will shoot at a given frequency.

For this, we'll use an interval operator to store new shots in the enemy value. We'll also introduce a new helper function, isVisible, that helps filter out elements whose coordinates are outside the visible screen. This is how the Enemy Observable looks now:

ch3/enemy_shots.js
```
function isVisible(obj) {
  return obj.x > -40 &&
    obj.x < canvas.width + 40 &&
    obj.y > -40 &&
    obj.y < canvas.height + 40;
}

const ENEMY_FREQ = 1500;
const ENEMY_SHOOTING_FREQ = 750;
const Enemies = Observable.interval(ENEMY_FREQ).scan(enemyArray => {
  const enemy = {
    x: parseInt(Math.random() * canvas.width),
    y: -30,
    shots: []
  };

  Observable.interval(ENEMY_SHOOTING_FREQ).subscribe(() => {
    enemy.shots.push({ x: enemy.x, y: enemy.y });
    enemy.shots = enemy.shots.filter(isVisible);
  });

  enemyArray.push(enemy);
  return enemyArray.filter(isVisible);
}, []);
```

In that code we create an interval every time we create a new enemy. This interval will keep adding shots to the enemy array of shots, and then it will filter out the ones outside the screen. We can use isVisible to filter out enemies that are outside the screen, too, as we do in the return statement.

We need to update paintEnemies so that it renders enemy shots and updates their y-coordinates. Then we use our handy drawTriangle function to draw the shots:

ch3/enemy_shots.js
```
function paintEnemies(enemies) {
  enemies.forEach(enemy => {
    enemy.y += 5;
    enemy.x += getRandomInt(-15, 15);

    drawTriangle(enemy.x, enemy.y, 20, '#00ff00', 'down');

➤   enemy.shots.forEach(shot => {
➤     shot.y += SHOOTING_SPEED;
➤     drawTriangle(shot.x, shot.y, 5, '#00ffff', 'down');
➤   });
  });
}
```

With this in place everybody is now shooting everybody else, but nobody is being destroyed! They simply glide past the enemies and our spaceship because we haven't defined what happens when shots collide with spaceships.

Managing Collisions

When a shot hits an enemy, we want both the shot and the enemy to disappear. Let's define a helper function to detect whether two targets have collided:

ch3/enemy_shots2.js
```
function collision(target1, target2) {
  return (
    target1.x > target2.x - 20 &&
    target1.x < target2.x + 20 &&
    (target1.y > target2.y - 20 && target1.y < target2.y + 20)
  );
}
```

Now let's modify the helper function paintHeroShots to check whether each shot hits an enemy. For cases where a hit occurs, we'll set a property isDead to true on the enemy that has been hit, and we'll set the coordinates of the shot to outside the screen. The shot will eventually be filtered out because it's outside the screen:

ch3/enemy_shots2.js
```
function paintEnemies(enemies) {
  enemies.forEach(enemy => {
    enemy.y += 5;
    enemy.x += getRandomInt(-15, 15);

➤   if (!enemy.isDead) {
➤     drawTriangle(enemy.x, enemy.y, 20, "#00ff00", "down");
➤   }

    enemy.shots.forEach(shot => {
      shot.y += SHOOTING_SPEED;
      drawTriangle(shot.x, shot.y, 5, "#00ffff", "down");
    });
```

```
    });
  }
  const SHOOTING_SPEED = 15;
  function paintHeroShots(heroShots, enemies) {
    heroShots.forEach((shot, i) => {
      for (const l = 0; l < enemies.length; l++) {
        const enemy = enemies[l];
➤       if (!enemy.isDead && collision(shot, enemy)) {
➤         enemy.isDead = true;
➤         shot.x = shot.y = -100;
➤         break;
➤       }
➤     }
      shot.y -= SHOOTING_SPEED;
      drawTriangle(shot.x, shot.y, 5, "#ffff00", "up");
    });
  }
```

Next let's get rid of any enemies that have the property isDead set to true. The only caveat is that we need to wait for all the shots from that particular enemy to disappear; otherwise, when we hit an enemy all its shots disappear along with it, which would be weird. So we check for the length of its shots and filter out the enemy object only when it has no shots left:

ch3/enemy_shots2.js
```
const Enemies = Observable.interval(ENEMY_FREQ).scan(enemyArray => {
  const enemy = {
    x: parseInt(Math.random() * canvas.width, 10),
    y: -30,
    shots: []
  };
  Observable.interval(ENEMY_SHOOTING_FREQ).subscribe(() => {
➤   if (!enemy.isDead) {
➤     enemy.shots.push({ x: enemy.x, y: enemy.y });
➤   }
    enemy.shots = enemy.shots.filter(isVisible);
  });
  enemyArray.push(enemy);
  return enemyArray
    .filter(isVisible)
➤   .filter(enemy => !(enemy.isDead && enemy.shots.length === 0));
}, []);
```

To check if the player's ship has been hit, we create a function gameOver:

ch3/enemy_shots2.js
```
function gameOver(ship, enemies) {
  return enemies.some(enemy => {
    if (collision(ship, enemy)) {
      return true;
    }

    return enemy.shots.some(shot => collision(ship, shot));
  });
}
```

This function returns true if an enemy or a shot from an enemy hits the player's spaceship.

Before moving on, let's get to know a useful operator: takeWhile. When we call takeWhile on an existing Observable, that Observable will keep emitting values until the function passed as a parameter to takeWhile returns false.

We can use takeWhile to tell our main combineLatest Observable to keep taking values until gameOver returns true:

ch3/enemy_shots2.js
```
Observable.combineLatest(
  StarStream,
  SpaceShip,
  Enemies,
  HeroShots,
  (stars, spaceship, enemies, heroShots) => ({
    stars,
    spaceship,
    enemies,
    heroShots
  })
)
  .sampleTime(SPEED)
➤ .takeWhile(actors => gameOver(actors.spaceship, actors.enemies) === false)
  .subscribe(renderScene);
```

When gameOver returns true, combineLatest will stop emitting values, effectively stopping the game.

One Last Thing: Keeping Score

What kind of game would it be if we couldn't brag to friends about our results? We obviously need a way to keep track of how well we did. We need a score.

Let's make a helper function to draw the score to the upper left of the screen:

ch3/score.js
```
function paintScore(score) {
  ctx.fillStyle = '#ffffff';
  ctx.font = 'bold 26px sans-serif';
  ctx.fillText(`Score: ${score}`, 40, 43);
}
```

To keep score we'll use a BehaviorSubject with a starting value of 0. We can easily use it in our combineLatest-based main game loop as if it were just another Observable, and we can push values to it whenever we want:

ch3/score.js
```
const ScoreSubject = new Rx.BehaviorSubject(0);
const score = ScoreSubject.scan((prev, cur) => prev + cur, 0);
```

In that code we use our friend the scan operator to sum each new value to the total aggregate result.

Now we just have to push the score to our Subject whenever we hit an enemy; that happens in paintHeroShots:

ch3/score.js
```
const SCORE_INCREASE = 10;
function paintHeroShots(heroShots, enemies) {
  heroShots.forEach((shot, i) => {
    for (let l = 0; l < enemies.length; l++) {
      const enemy = enemies[l];
      if (!enemy.isDead && collision(shot, enemy)) {
        ScoreSubject.next(SCORE_INCREASE);
        enemy.isDead = true;
        shot.x = shot.y = -100;
        break;
      }
    }

    shot.y -= SHOOTING_SPEED;
    drawTriangle(shot.x, shot.y, 5, '#ffff00', 'up');
  });
}
```

And of course, we add paintScore to renderScene so the score appears onscreen:

ch3/score.js
```
function renderScene(actors) {
  paintStars(actors.stars);
  paintSpaceShip(actors.spaceship.x, actors.spaceship.y);
  paintEnemies(actors.enemies);
  paintHeroShots(actors.heroShots, actors.enemies);
  paintScore(actors.score);
}
```

That completes our Spaceship Reactive game. With about 200 lines we've managed to code an entire game in the browser, avoiding changing any external state through the power of Observable pipelines.

Ideas for Improvements

I'm sure you already have some ideas for making the game even more exciting, but let me offer some suggestions that will improve the game and sharpen your RxJS skills at the same time:

- Add a second (or third!) star field that moves at a different speed to create a parallax effect. This could be done in several different ways. Try to reuse existing code and to do it as declaratively as you can.

- Increase the intensity of the game by getting the enemies to act more unpredictably—for example, by making them fire at random intervals instead of the fixed one specified in ENEMY_SHOOTING_FREQ. Extra points if you can get them to fire more quickly as the player's score gets higher!

- Allow the player to get more points by hitting several enemies in a short amount of time.

Wrapping Up

We've built an entire game for the browser using only Observables, and along the way we've seen several extremely convenient methods to handle concurrency and to compose and transform Observables. This is one of the strengths of RxJS: there is always a method to help with the problem you're trying to tackle. Feel free to explore them in the RxJS documentation.[1]

Reactive programming makes it easy to write concurrent programs. The Observable abstraction and the powerful RxJS methods make it natural for different parts of a program to interact efficiently. Programming without relying on external state might take some getting used to, but it has enormous benefits. We can encapsulate entire behaviors in a single Observable pipeline, making our program more solid and reliable.

In the next chapter we'll pick up our earthquake visualizer application from where we left it and add a Node.js server part that shows tweets related to the earthquakes. We'll also improve its user interface to make it look like a real earthquake dashboard.

---

1. https://github.com/Reactive-Extensions/RxJS/blob/master/doc/api/core/observable.md

CHAPTER 4

Building a Complete Web Application

In this chapter we'll build a typical web application, using RxJS in the front end and back end. We'll transform the Document Object Model (DOM) and do client-server communication using WebSockets in a Node.js server.

For the server back-end, we'll use two well-established node libraries and wrap some of their APIs with Observables to use them in our application.

After this chapter, you'll be able to use RxJS to build user interfaces in a declarative way, using the techniques we've seen so far and applying them to the DOM. You'll also be ready to use RxJS in any Node.js project and able to use reactive programming and RxJS in any project.

Building a Real-Time Earthquake Dashboard

We'll be creating both server and client parts for an earthquake dashboard application, building on the application we started in *Making a Real-Time Earthquake Visualizer*, on page 29. We'll build the server in Node.js, and improve our application to make it more interactive and informative.

The screenshot on page 70 shows how the dashboard will look when we're finished.

Our starting point will be the code from *Making a Real-Time Earthquake Visualizer*, on page 29, which we left like this:

```
ch2/earthquake-visualizer/src/index.js
const quakes$ = Observable.interval(5000)
  .flatMap(() => {
    return loadJSONP({
      url: QUAKE_URL,
      callbackName: "eqfeed_callback"
    }).retry(3);
  })
```

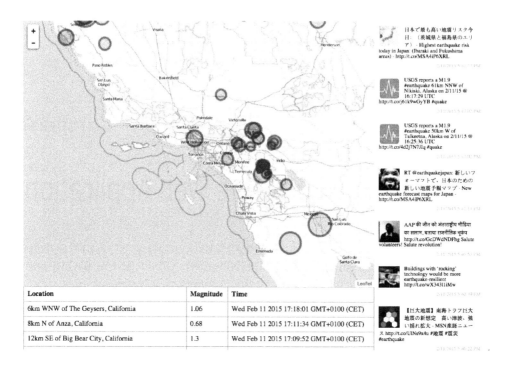

Location	Magnitude	Time
6km WNW of The Geysers, California	1.06	Wed Feb 11 2015 17:18:01 GMT+0100 (CET)
8km N of Anza, California	0.68	Wed Feb 11 2015 17:11:34 GMT+0100 (CET)
12km SE of Big Bear City, California	1.3	Wed Feb 11 2015 17:09:52 GMT+0100 (CET)

```
  .flatMap(result => Observable.from(result.response.features))
  .distinct(quake => quake.properties.code);

quakes$.subscribe(quake => {
  const coords = quake.geometry.coordinates;
  const size = quake.properties.mag * 10000;

  L.circle([coords[1], coords[0]], size).addTo(map);
});
```

This code already has one potential bug: it could be executed before the DOM is ready, throwing errors whenever we try to use the DOM in our code. We want to load our code after the DOMContentLoaded event is fired, which signals that the browser is aware of all the elements on the page.

We can use the Rx.Observable.fromEvent operator to listen to the DOMContentLoaded event and run our code only when the DOM is ready:

ch4/earthquake-visualizer/src/1_domready.js
```
import { Observable } from "rxjs/Observable";
import L from "leaflet";

const QUAKE_URL = `http://earthquake.usgs.gov/earthquakes/
feed/v1.0/summary/all_day.geojson`;
```

```
function initialize() {
  const quakes$ = Observable
    .interval(5000)
    .flatMap(() => {
      return loadJSONP({
        url: QUAKE_URL,
        callbackName: "eqfeed_callback"
      }).retry(3);
    })
    .flatMap(result => Observable.from(result.response.features))
    .distinct(quake => quake.properties.code);

  quakes$.subscribe(quake => {
    const coords = quake.geometry.coordinates;
    const size = quake.properties.mag * 10000;

    L.circle([coords[1], coords[0]], size).addTo(map);
  });
}
Observable.fromEvent(document, "DOMContentLoaded").subscribe(initialize);
```

Next, we'll add an empty table to our HTML template, which is where we'll populate earthquake data in the next section:

```
<table>
  <thead>
    <tr>
      <th>Location</th>
      <th>Magnitude</th>
      <th>Time</th>
    </tr>
  </thead>
  <tbody id="quakes_info">
  </tbody>
</table>
```

With this, we're ready to start writing new code for our dashboard.

Adding a List of Earthquakes

The first feature is to display a real-time list of earthquakes, including information about their locations, magnitudes, and dates. The data for this list is the same as for the map, which comes from the USGS website. We'll first create a function that returns a row element given a props object parameter:

```
ch4/earthquake-visualizer/src/2_rows.js
function makeRow(props) {
  const row = document.createElement("tr");
  row.id = props.net + props.code;
```

```
const time = new Date(props.time).toString();

[props.place, props.mag, time].forEach(text => {
  const cell = document.createElement("td");
  cell.textContent = text;
  row.appendChild(cell);
});

return row;
}
```

The props parameter is the same as the properties property in the JSON that we retrieve from the USGS site.

To generate the rows, we'll make another subscription to the quakes$ Observable. This subscription creates a row in the table for each new earthquake received. We add the code at the end of the initialize function:

ch4/earthquake-visualizer/src/2_rows.js
```
const table = document.getElementById("quakes_info");
quakes$.pluck("properties").map(makeRow).subscribe(table.appendChild);
```

The pluck operator extracts the value of properties from each earthquake object, because it contains all the info we need for makeRow. Then we map each earthquake object to makeRow to transform it into a populated HTML tr element. Finally, in the subscription we append every emitted row to our table.

This should give us a nicely populated table whenever we receive the earthquake data.

Looks good, and it was easy enough! Still, we can make some improvements. First, though, we need to explore an important concept in RxJS: hot and cold Observables.

Hot and Cold Observables

The concepts "hot" and "cold" when applied to Observables are often a topic of confusion in the Rx world, but they are actually easy to grasp. "Hot" Observables emit values regardless of having any Subscribers. On the other hand, "cold" Observables emit the entire sequence of values from the start to every Subscriber.

Hot Observables

Any Subscriber subscribed to a hot Observable will receive values emitted only from the exact moment it subscribes to it. Every other Subscriber subscribed at that moment will receive the exact same values. This is similar to how JavaScript events work.

Mouse events and a stock-exchange ticker are examples of hot Observables. In both cases the Observable emits values regardless of whether it has Subscribers, and could already be producing values before any Subscriber is listening. Here's an example:

```
const onMove = Observable.fromEvent(document, "mousemove");
onMove.subscribe(e => {
  console.log(`Subscription 1: ${e.clientX} ${e.clientY}`);
});
onMove.subscribe(e => {
  console.log(`Subscription 2: ${e.clientX} ${e.clientY}`);
});

// Result:
// Subscription 1: 23 24
// Subscription 2: 23 24
// Subscription 1: 34 37
// Subscription 2: 34 37
// Subscription 1: 46 49
// Subscription 2: 46 49
// ...
```

In the example, both Subscribers receive the same values from the Observable as they are emitted. To JavaScript programmers, that behavior feels natural because it resembles how JavaScript events work.

Now let's see how cold Observables work.

Cold Observables

A cold Observable emits values only when Subscribers subscribe to it.

For example, Rx.Observable.range returns a cold Observable. Every new Subscriber that subscribes to it will receive the whole range:

```
function printValue(value) {
  console.log(value);
}

const rangeToFive = Observable.range(1, 5);
const obs1 = rangeToFive.subscribe(printValue); // 1, 2, 3, 4, 5
const obs2 = Observable.of().delay(2000).flatMap(() => {
  // Creates an empty Observable
  return rangeToFive.subscribe(printValue); // 1, 2, 3, 4, 5
});
```

Understanding when we're dealing with hot or cold Observables is essential to avoid subtle and sneaky bugs. For example, Rx.Observable.interval returns an Observable that produces an increasing integer value at regular intervals of time. Imagine we want to use it to push the same values to several Subscribers. We could implement it like this:

```
const source = Observable.interval(2000);
source.subscribe(x => {
  console.log(`Subscription 1, next value: ${x}`);
});

source.subscribe(x => {
  console.log(`Subscription 2: next value: ${x}`);
});
```

Output:

```
Subscription 1, next value: 0
Subscription 2: next value: 0
Subscription 1, next value: 1
Subscription 2: next value: 1
...
```

That seems to work. But now imagine that we need the second Subscriber to join three seconds after the first one:

```
const source = Observable.interval(1000);
source.subscribe(x => {
  console.log(`Subscription 1: ${x}`);
});

setTimeout(() => {
  source.subscribe(x => {
    console.log(`Subscription 2: ${x}`);
  });
}, 3000);
```

Output:

```
Subscription 1: 0
Subscription 1: 1
Subscription 1: 2
Subscription 1: 3
Subscription 2: 0
Subscription 1: 4
Subscription 2: 1
...
```

Now we see that something is really off. When subscribing three seconds later, the second subscription receives all the values that the source already pushed, instead of starting with the current value and continuing from there, because Rx.Observable.interval is a *cold* Observable. If the difference between hot and cold Observables is not clear, scenarios like this can be surprising.

If we have several Subscribers listening to a cold Observable, they will receive copies of the same sequence of values. So strictly speaking, although the Subscribers are sharing the same Observable, they are not sharing the same exact sequence of values. If we want the Subscribers to share the same sequence, we need a hot Observable.

From Cold to Hot Using publish

We can turn a cold Observable into a hot one using publish. Calling publish creates a new Observable that acts as a proxy to the original one. It does that by subscribing itself to the original and pushing the values it receives to its Subscribers.

A *published* Observable is actually a ConnectableObservable, which has an extra method called connect that we call to start receiving values. This allows us to subscribe to it before it starts running:

```
// Create an Observable that yields a value every second
const source = Observable.interval(1000);
const publisher = source.publish();

// Even if we are subscribing, no values are pushed yet.
publisher.subscribe(x => {
  console.log(`Subscription 1: ${x}`);
});

// publisher connects and starts publishing values
publisher.connect();

setTimeout(() => {
  // Five seconds later, we subscribe to it and start receiving
  // current values, not the whole sequence.
  publisher.subscribe(x => {
    console.log(`Subscription 2: ${x}`);
  });
}, 5000);
```

Sharing a Cold Observable

Let's get back to our earthquake example. The code we have so far looks reasonable; we have an Observable quakes$ with two subscriptions: one that paints earthquakes on the map, and one that lists them in the table.

But we can make our code much more efficient. By having two Subscribers to quakes$ we're, in fact, requesting the data twice. You can check that by putting a console.log inside the flatMap operator in quakes$.

This happens because quakes$ is a cold Observable, and it will re-emit all its values to each new Subscriber, so a new subscription means a new JSONP request. This impacts our application performance by requesting the same resources twice over the network.

For the next example we'll use the share operator, which automatically creates a subscription to the Observable when the number of Subscribers goes from zero to one. This spares us from calling connect:

ch4/earthquake-visualizer/src/2_rows.js
```js
const quakes$ = Observable.interval(5000)
  .flatMap(() => {
    return loadJSONP({
      url: QUAKE_URL,
      callbackName: "eqfeed_callback"
    }).retry(3);
  })
  .flatMap(result => Observable.from(result.response.features))
  .distinct(quake => quake.properties.code)
  .share();
```

Now quakes$ behaves like a hot Observable, and we don't have to worry about how many Subscribers we connect to it, since they will all receive the exact same data.

Buffering Values

Our preceding code works well, but notice that we insert a tr node every time we receive information about an earthquake. That's inefficient, because with each insertion we're modifying the DOM and causing a repaint of the page, making the browser do unnecessary work to calculate the new layout. This can cause noticeable performance drop.

Ideally, we would batch several incoming earthquake objects and insert each batch every few seconds. That would be tricky to implement by hand because we'd have to keep counters and element buffers, and we would have to remember to reset them with every batch. But with RxJS we can just use one of the buffer-based RxJS operators, like bufferTime.

With bufferTime we can buffer incoming values and release them as an array every *x* period of time:

ch4/earthquake-visualizer/src/code3.bufferWithTime.js
```js
const table = document.getElementById("quakes_info");
quakes$
  .pluck("properties")
  .map(makeRow)
  .bufferTime(500)
```

```
      .filter(rows => rows.length > 0) // )
      .map(rows => {
        const fragment = document.createDocumentFragment();
        rows.forEach(row => {
          fragment.appendChild(row);
        });
        return fragment;
      })
      .subscribe(fragment => {
        table.appendChild(fragment);
      });
```

This is what's going on in the new code:

❶ Buffer every incoming value and release the batch of values every 500 milliseconds.

❷ bufferTime executes every 500ms no matter what, and if there have been no incoming values, it will yield an empty array. We'll filter those.

❸ We insert every row into a *document fragment*, which is a document without a parent. This means it's not in the DOM, and modifying its contents is very fast and efficient.

❹ Finally, we append the fragment to the DOM. An advantage of appending a fragment is that it counts as a single operation, causing just one redraw. It also appends the fragment's children to the same element to which we're appending the fragment itself.

Using buffers and fragments, we manage to keep row insertion performant while keeping the real-time nature of our application (with a maximum delay of half a second). Now we're ready to add the next feature to our dashboard: interactivity!

Adding Interaction

We now have earthquakes on the map and in a list, but no interaction between both representations yet. It would be nice, for example, to center an earthquake on the map whenever we click it on the list, and to highlight an earthquake with a circle on the map when we move the mouse over its row. Let's get to it.

We can use the Leaflet library introduced in Chapter 2 to draw on a map, and put drawings in their own layers so you can manipulate them individually. Let's create a group of layers called quakeLayer where we'll store all the earthquake circles. Each circle will be a layer inside the group. We'll also create an object codeLayers where we'll store the correlation between an earthquake code and the internal layer ID, so that we can refer to circles by the earthquake ID:

ch4/earthquake-visualizer/src/3_draw.js
```
const codeLayers = {};
const quakeLayer = L.layerGroup([]).addTo(map);
```

And now in the subscription for the quakes$ Observable inside initialize, we'll add each circle to the layer group and store its ID in codeLayers (if this seems a bit intricate, it's because that's the only way Leaflet allows us to refer to drawings in a map):

ch4/earthquake-visualizer/src/3_draw.js
```
quakes$.subscribe(quake => {
  const coords = quake.geometry.coordinates;
  const size = quake.properties.mag * 10000;

  const circle = L.circle([coords[1], coords[0]], size).addTo(map);
  quakeLayer.addLayer(circle);
  codeLayers[quake.id] = quakeLayer.getLayerId(circle);
});
```

Let's now create the hovering effect. We'll write a new function, isHovering, which returns an Observable that emits a Boolean value for whether the mouse is over a particular earthquake circle at any given moment:

ch4/earthquake-visualizer/src/3_draw.js
```
❶ const identity = x => x;

function isHovering(element) {
❷   const over = Observable.fromEvent(element, "mouseover").map(identity(true));
❸   const out = Observable.fromEvent(element, "mouseout").map(identity(false));

❹   return over.merge(out);
}
```

❶ This is the identity function. Given a parameter x, it returns x.

❷ over is an Observable that emits true when the user hovers the mouse over the element.

❸ out is an Observable that emits false when the user moves the mouse outside of the element.

❹ isHovering merges both over and out, returning an Observable that emits true when the mouse is over an element, and false when it leaves it.

With isHovering in place we can modify the subscription that creates the rows, so that we subscribe to events in each row as it is created:

ch4/earthquake-visualizer/src/3_draw.js

```
const table = document.getElementById("quakes_info");
quakes$
  .pluck("properties")
  .map(makeRow)
  .bufferTime(500)
  .filter(rows => rows.length > 0)
  .map(rows => {
    const fragment = document.createDocumentFragment();
    rows.forEach(row => {
      const circle = quakeLayer.getLayer(codeLayers[row.id]);

      isHovering(row).subscribe(hovering => {
        circle.setStyle({
          color: hovering ? "#ff0000" : "#0000ff"
        });
      });

      Observable.fromEvent(row, "click").subscribe(() => {
        map.panTo(circle.getLatLng());
      });

      fragment.appendChild(row);
    });
    return fragment;
  })
  .subscribe(fragment => {
    table.appendChild(fragment);
  });
```

❶ We get the circle element for the earthquake on the map using the ID we get from the row element. With that, codeLayers gives us the corresponding internal ID, which gets us the circle element using quakeLayer.getLayer.

❷ We call isHovering with the current row and we subscribe to the resulting Observable. If the hovering argument is true, we'll paint the circle red; otherwise, it will be blue.

❸ We subscribe to the Observable created from the click event in the current row. When the row in the list is clicked, the map will be centered on the corresponding circle in the map.

Making It Efficient

Experienced front-end developers know that creating many events on a page is a recipe for bad performance. In our previous example, we created three events for each row. If we get 100 earthquakes on the list, we would have 300 events floating around the page just to do some light highlighting work! That is terrible for performance, and we can do better.

Events in the DOM always bubble up (from children to parent elements), so a technique to avoid attaching events to elements individually is attaching them to their parent element instead. Once the event is fired on the parent, we can use the event's target property to find the child element that was the actual target.

Because we'll need similar functionality for the events click and mouseover, we'll create a function getRowFromEvent:

ch4/earthquake-visualizer/src/code3.pairwise.js
```
function getRowFromEvent(event) {
  return Observable
    .fromEvent(table, event)
    .filter({target} => {
      return target.tagName === "TD" && target.parentNode.id.length;
    })
    .pluck("target", "parentNode")
    .distinctUntilChanged();
}
```

❶
❷
❸

getRowFromEvent gives us the table row in which the event has happened. Here are the details:

❶ We make sure that we get events happening in a table cell, and we check that the parent of that cell is a row with an ID attribute. These rows are the ones we tagged with the earthquake ID.

❷ The pluck operator extracts the nested property parentNode inside the element's target property.

❸ This prevents getting the same element more than once. That would happen a lot with the mouseover event, for example.

In the previous section we attached the events mouseover and mouseout on each row to change the earthquake circle color each time the mouse entered or exited the row. Now, we'll use only the mouseover event on the table, combined with the convenient pairwise operator:

ch4/earthquake-visualizer/src/code3.pairwise.js
```
getRowFromEvent("mouseover").pairwise().subscribe(rows => {
  const prevCircle = quakeLayer.getLayer(codeLayers[rows[0].id]);
  const currCircle = quakeLayer.getLayer(codeLayers[rows[1].id]);

  prevCircle.setStyle({ color: "#0000ff" });
  currCircle.setStyle({ color: "#ff0000" });
});
```

pairwise groups each emitted value with the previously emitted value in an array. Because we're always getting distinct rows, pairwise will always yield the row that the mouse just left and the row where the mouse is hovering now. With this information, it is easy to color each earthquake circle accordingly.

Handling the click event is even simpler:

ch4/earthquake-visualizer/src/code3.pairwise.js
```
getRowFromEvent("click").subscribe(row => {
  const circle = quakeLayer.getLayer(codeLayers[row.id]);
  map.panTo(circle.getLatLng());
});
```

And we can go back to just subscribing to quakes$ to generate the rows:

ch4/earthquake-visualizer/src/code3.pairwise.js
```
quakes$
  .pluck("properties")
  .map(makeRow)
  .subscribe(table.appendChild);
```

Our code is now much more clean and idiomatic, and it doesn't depend on the rows being there. If there are no rows, getRowFromEvent won't try to yield any.

What's more important, our code now is very efficient. Regardless of the amount of earthquake information we retrieve, we'll always have just a single mouseover event and a single click event, instead of hundreds of events.

Getting Real-Time Updates from Twitter

The second part of our plan to make a real-time dashboard for earthquakes is to add reports and information from Twitter related to the different earthquakes happening on the planet. For this, we'll create a small Node.js program that will fetch the stream of tweets related to the earthquakes.

Setting Up Our Node.js Environment

Let's configure our Node.js application. Besides RxJS, we will be using two venerable third-party modules to make our life easier: ws and twit.[1] Any similar modules should work with minimal changes to the code.

First, let's create a folder for our application and install the modules that we'll use (note that the output of the npm command may vary depending on the current versions of the packages):

---

1.   https://github.com/websockets/ws and https://github.com/ttezel/twit

```
~$ mkdir tweet_stream
~$ cd tweet_stream
~/tweet_stream$ npm install ws twit rxjs
  code@1.0.0 /Users/sergi/code/tweet_stream
  ├─┬ rxjs@5.2.0
  │ └── symbol-observable@1.0.4
  ├─┬ twit@2.2.5
  │ ├── bluebird@3.5.0
  │ └── request@2.80.0
  └─┬ ws@2.2.0
    └── ultron@1.1.0
```

Client–Server Communication

Now we're ready to start building our application. Let's create a new file called index.js inside the tweet_stream folder to load the modules we'll use:

ch4/tweet_stream/index.js
```
const WebSocket = require("ws");
const Twit = require("twit");
const Rx = require("rxjs");
const Observable = Rx.Observable;
```

To use the Twitter API, you need to request a consumer key and an access token from the Twitter website. Once you have that, create a new Twit object with a configuration object, like this:

ch4/tweet_stream/index.js
```
const T = new Twit({
  // Substitute the following properties by the ones provided by Twitter
  consumer_key: "xxxxxxxxxxxxxxxxxxxxxxxxxxxxxx",
  consumer_secret: "xxxxxxxxxxxxxxxxxxxxxxxxxxxxxx",
  access_token: "xxxxxxxxxxxxxxxxxxxxxxxxxxxxxx",
  access_token_secret: "xxxxxxxxxxxxxxxxxxxxxxxxxxxxxx"
});
```

Now we can create a function, onConnect, that will do all the work of searching tweets and communicating with the client in the future, and we can initiate a WebSocket server that will call onConnect once the WebSocket is connected and ready:

ch4/tweet_stream/index.js
```
function onConnect(ws) {
  console.log('Client connected on localhost:8080');
}

const Server = new WebSocketServer({ port: 8080 });
Observable.fromEvent(Server, 'connection').subscribe(onConnect);
```

We can now launch our application, and it should start a WebSocket connection on port 8080:

```
~/tweet_stream$ node index.js
```

The message about a client connection is not printed yet because we haven't connected any browser to this server. Let's now switch to the code for our dashboard and do that. We'll use the webSocket:

ch4/earthquake-visualizer/src/4_websocket.js
```
function initialize() {
  const socket$ = Observable.webSocket("ws://127.0.0.1:8080");
  ...
```

In the preceding code, webSocket creates a Subject that serves as the sender and receiver of messages to the WebSocket server. By calling socket$.onNext we'll be able to send messages to the server, and by subscribing to socket$ we'll receive any messages the server sends us.

We can now send the server messages with the earthquake data we receive:

ch4/earthquake-visualizer/src/4_websocket.js
```
quakes$.bufferCount(100).subscribe(quakes => {
  const quakesData = quakes.map(quake => ({
    id: quake.properties.net + quake.properties.code,
    lat: quake.geometry.coordinates[1],
    lng: quake.geometry.coordinates[0],
    mag: quake.properties.mag
  }));
  socket$.next(JSON.stringify({ quakes: quakesData }));
});
```

And we can set up a Subscriber for messages coming from the server:

ch4/earthquake-visualizer/src/4_websocket.js
```
socket$.subscribe(message => {
  console.log(JSON.parse(message.data));
});
```

Now when we reload the browser, the client message should appear in the terminal:

```
~/tweet_stream$ node index.js
Client connected on localhost:8080
```

Fantastic! The browser should be sending commands to the server as soon as it starts receiving earthquakes from the remote JSONP resource. For now, the server completely ignores those messages, though. Time to go back to our tweet stream code and do something with them.

First we'll connect to the message events that arrive to the server from the browser client. Whenever the client sends a message, the WebSocket server emits a message event with the contents of the message. In our case, the contents are a stringified object.

We can write the following code in our onConnect function:

```
ch4/tweet_stream/index.js
const onMessage = Observable.fromEvent(ws, 'message')
  .subscribe(quake => {
    quake = JSON.parse(quake);
    console.log(quake);
  });
```

If we restart the server (Ctrl-C in the terminal) and reload the browser, we should see the earthquake details being printed in the terminal as they come in. That's perfect. Now we're ready to start looking for tweets related to our earthquakes.

Retrieving and Sending Tweets

We're using the streaming Twitter client for Node.js twit to connect to Twitter and search tweets. All the code in the server from now on will happen inside the onConnect function because it assumes that a connection to a WebSocket is already established. Let's initialize the stream of tweets:

```
ch4/tweet_stream/index.js
const stream = T.stream("statuses/filter", {
  track: "earthquake",
  locations: []
});
```

This tells our Twit instance T to start streaming Twitter statuses, filtered by the keyword earthquake. This is, of course, very generic and not that directly related to the earthquakes happening right now. But notice the empty locations array. This is an array of latitude and longitude boundaries that we can use to filter tweets by their geographic location, along with the word *earthquake*. That's much more specific! Alright, let's subscribe to this stream and start sending tweets to the browser:

```
ch4/tweet_stream/index.js
Observable.fromEvent(stream, "tweet").subscribe(tweetObject => {
  ws.send(JSON.stringify(tweetObject), err => {
    if (err) {
      console.log("There was an error sending the message");
    }
  });
});
```

If we restart the server and reload the browser, we should receive tweets in the browser, and the console in the development panel should be printing the tweets.

These tweets are not filtered by earthquake location yet. To do that, we need to do the following things with each piece of earthquake information we receive:

- Take the longitude and latitude pair of epicenter coordinates of each earthquake and create a bounding box that delimits the geographical area of the tweets that we consider related to the earthquake.

- Accumulate all the boundary coordinates so that tweets sent to the client keep being relevant to the earthquakes on the map.

- Update the twit stream with the new coordinates every time we receive the message for a new earthquake.

Here's a way to do it:

```
ch4/tweet_stream/index.js
Observable.fromEvent(ws, "message")
  .flatMap(quakesObj => {
    quakesObj = JSON.parse(quakesObj);
    return Observable.from(quakesObj.quakes);
  })
① .scan([], (boundsArray, quake) => {
②   const bounds = [
      quake.lng - 0.3,
      quake.lat - 0.15,
      quake.lng + 0.3,
      quake.lat + 0.15
    ].map(
      coordinate => coordinate.toString().match(/\-?\d+(\.\-?\d{2})?/)[0]
    );

    const finalBounds = boundsArray.concat(bounds);
③   return finalBounds.slice(Math.max(finalBounds.length - 50, 0));
  })
④ .subscribe(boundsArray => {
    stream.stop();
    stream.params.locations = boundsArray;
    stream.start();
  });
```

And here is the step-by-step of what is happening in the preceding code:

❶ We meet our old friend scan again. Any time we need to accumulate results and yield each intermediate result, scan is our friend. In this case, we'll keep accumulating earthquake coordinates in the boundsArray array.

❷ From the single latitude/longitude pair of coordinates of the epicenter of the earthquake, we create an array that contains an area determined by a north-west coordinate and a south-east one. The numbers used to approximate the bounds create a rectangle the size of a large city.

After creating the array, we use a regular expression to limit the decimal precision of each coordinate to two decimals, to comply with the Twitter API requirements.

❸ We concatenate the generated boundaries to boundsArray, which contains every previous earthquake's boundaries. Then we take the last 25 pairs of boundaries (50 items in the array), since that is the limit of the Twitter API.

❹ Finally, we subscribe to the Observable, and in the onNext function we restart the current twit stream to reload the updated locations to filter by with our new accumulated array of locations, converted to a string.

After restarting the server and reloading the browser, we should be receiving relevant tweets in our browser application. For now, we can only see the raw objects displayed in the developer console, though. In the next section we generate the HTML to display the tweets in our dashboard.

Showing Tweets on the Dashboard

Now that we're receiving tweets from the server, the only thing left to do is show them nicely on the screen. For this, we'll create a new HTML element in the template where we append incoming tweets:

ch4/earthquake-visualizer/template.html
```
<div id="tweet_container"></div>
```

We will also update our socket Observable subscription to process the incoming tweet objects and append them to the tweet_container element that we just created:

ch4/earthquake-visualizer/src/5_show_tweets.js
```
socket
  .map(message => {
    console.log(message.data);
    JSON.parse(message.data);
  })
  .subscribe(data => {
    const container = document.getElementById("tweet_container");
    container.insertBefore(makeTweetElement(data), container.firstChild);
  });
```

Any new tweets will appear at the top of the list, and they will be created by makeTweetElement, a simple function that creates a tweet element and populates it with the data we pass as a parameter:

ch4/earthquake-visualizer/src/5_show_tweets.js
```
function makeTweetElement(tweetObj) {
  const tweetEl = document.createElement("div");
  tweetEl.className = "tweet";

  const time = new Date(tweetObj.created_at);
  const timeText = `${time.toLocaleDateString()} ${time.toLocaleTimeString()}`;

  tweetEl.innerHTML = `
    <img src="${tweetObj.user.profile_image_url}" class="avatar" />
      <div class="content">${tweetObj.text}</div>
    <div class="time">${timeText}</div>`;

  return tweetEl;
}
```

And with this we finally have a sidebar with relevant, geolocated tweets that can give us more insight about the areas affected by the earthquakes.

Ideas for Improvements

This dashboard is already functional, but there are many improvements that could be done. Some ideas to make it better:

- Add more earthquake databases. USGS is a fantastic resource, but it mainly focuses on earthquakes happening in the United States. It would be interesting to merge in earthquake reports from around the world, not just the United States, and present them all together in the map. To do this, you could utilize merge and mergeAll, and use distinct with a selector function to avoid duplicates.

- Whenever the user clicks on a tweet, center the map on the related earthquake. This would involve grouping the tweets by earthquake on the server, and you'd probably want to use the groupBy operator to group tweets to a particular geographical area.

Wrapping Up

In this chapter we've used RxJS to create a reactive user interface that allows us to see different kinds of data about earthquakes happening on the planet in real time. We've used RxJS both in the browser client and in the Node.js server, showing how easy it is to use Observables to manage different areas of an application.

More importantly, we've seen that we can use RxJS in the same way on the client and on the server, bringing the Observable sequence abstraction everywhere in our application. And not only that. We could actually use RxJS concepts and operators across other programming languages, since RxJS is supported in many of them.

Next we'll look at *Schedulers*, a more advanced object type in RxJS that allows us to control time and concurrency with more precision, and provides a great help with testing our code.

CHAPTER 5

Bending Time with Schedulers

As soon as I discovered RxJS, I started using it in my projects. For a while I thought I knew how to use it effectively, but there was a nagging question: how do I know whether the operator I'm using is synchronous or asynchronous? In other words, when exactly do operators emit notifications? This seemed a crucial part of using RxJS correctly, but it felt a bit blurry to me.

The interval operator, I thought, is clearly asynchronous, so it must use something like setTimeout internally to emit items. But what if I'm using range? Does it emit asynchronously as well? Does it block the event loop? What about from? I was using these operators everywhere, but I didn't know much about their internal concurrency model.

Then I learned about Schedulers.

Schedulers are a powerful mechanism to precisely manage concurrency in your applications. They give you fine-grained control over how an Observable emits notifications by allowing you to change their concurrency model as you go. In this chapter you'll learn how to use Schedulers and apply them in common scenarios. We'll focus on testing, where Schedulers are especially useful, and you'll learn how to make your own Schedulers.

Using Schedulers

A Scheduler is a mechanism to "schedule" an action to happen in the future. Each operator in RxJS uses one Scheduler internally, selected to provide the best performance in the most likely scenario.

Let's see how we can change the Scheduler in operators and the consequences of doing so. First let's create an array with 1,000 integers in it:

```
const itemArray = [];
for (let i = 0; i < 1000; i++) {
  itemArray.push(i);
}
```

Then, we create an Observable from arr and force it to emit all the notifications by subscribing to it. In the code we also measure the amount of time it takes to emit all the notifications:

```
const timeStart = Date.now();
Observable.from(itemArray).subscribe(null, null, () => {
  console.log(`Total time: ${Date.now() - timeStart}ms`);
});
```

❮ "Total time: 1ms"

One millisecond—not bad! Unlike RxJS 4, RxJS 5 doesn't use any Scheduler by default, so this code processes all the notifications synchronously.

Now let's change the Scheduler to Rx.Scheduler.asap:

```
const timeStart = Date.now();
Observable.from(itemArray, Scheduler.asap).subscribe(null, null, () => {
  console.log(`Total time: ${Date.now() - timeStart}ms`);
});
```

❮ "Total time: 169ms"

Wow, our code runs more than a hundred times slower than with no Scheduler. That's because the asap Scheduler runs each notification asynchronously. We can verify this by adding a simple log statement after the subscription.

Using no Scheduler:

```
Rx.Observable.from(arr).subscribe( ... );
console.log('Hi there!');
```

❮ "Total time: 1ms"
  "Hi there!"

Using the asap Scheduler:

```
Rx.Observable.from(arr, Rx.Scheduler.asap).subscribe( ... );
console.log('Hi there!');
```

❮ "Hi there!"
  "Total time: 169ms"

When using no Scheduler, the console.log statement happens only when the Observable has emitted all of its notifications, because they happen synchronously. But when Rx.Scheduler.asap is used, console.log runs first, whereas our Observer's notifications run asynchronously, so they appear after the console.log statement.

So, Schedulers have a big impact on how our Observables work. In our case here, performance suffered from asynchronously processing a big, already-available array. But we can use Schedulers to improve performance. For example, we can switch the Scheduler on the fly before doing expensive operations on an Observable:

```
Observable.from(itemArray)
  .groupBy(value => value % 2 === 0)
  .map(value => value.observeOn(Scheduler.asap))
  .map(groupedObservable => expensiveOperation(groupedObservable));
```

In the preceding code we group all the values in the array into two groups: even and uneven values. groupBy returns an Observable that emits an Observable for each group created. And here's the cool part: just before running an expensive operation on the items in each grouped Observable, we use observeOn to switch the Scheduler to the asap one, so that the expensive operation will be executed asynchronously, not blocking the event loop.

observeOn and subscribeOn

In the previous section, we used the observeOn operator to change the Scheduler in some Observables. observeOn and subscribeOn are instance operators that return a copy of the Observable instance, but that use the Scheduler we pass as a parameter.

observeOn takes a Scheduler and returns a new Observable that uses that Scheduler. It will make every next call run in the new Scheduler.

subscribeOn forces the subscription and un-subscription work (not the notifications) of an Observable to run on a particular Scheduler. Like observeOn, it accepts a Scheduler as a parameter. subscribeOn is useful when, for example, we're running in the browser and doing significant work in the subscribe call but we don't want to block the UI thread with it.

Basic Rx Schedulers

Let's look a bit more in depth at the Schedulers that we just used. The ones RxJS's operators use the most are asap and queue. There are other, more specialized Schedulers like the animationFrame scheduler, which we wll see later in the chapter.

The asap Scheduler

The asap Scheduler runs actions asynchronously. You can think of it as a rough equivalent of setTimeout with zero milliseconds delay that keeps the order in the sequence. It uses the most efficient asynchronous implementation available on the platform it runs (for example, process.nextTick in Node.js or set-Timeout in the browser).

Let's take the previous example with range and make it run on the asap Scheduler. For this, we'll use the observeOn operator:

```
console.log("Before subscription");
Observable.range(1, 5)
  .do(value => {
    console.log("Processing value", value);
  })
  .observeOn(Scheduler.asap)
  .map(value => value * value)
  .subscribe(value => {
    console.log("Emitted", value);
  });
console.log("After subscription");
```

```
❮ Before subscription
  Processing value 1
  Processing value 2
  Processing value 3
  Processing value 4
  Processing value 5
  After subscription
  Emitted 1
  Emitted 4
  Emitted 9
  Emitted 16
  Emitted 25
```

There are significant differences in the output this time. Our console.log statement runs immediately for every value, but we make the Observable run on the asap Scheduler, which yields each value asynchronously. That means our log statements in the do operator are processed before the squared values.

When to Use It

The asap Scheduler never blocks the event loop, so it's ideal for operations that involve time, like asynchronous requests. It can also be used in Observables that never complete, because it doesn't block the program while waiting for new notifications that may never happen.

The queue Scheduler

The queue Scheduler is synchronous like the immediate Scheduler. The difference is that if we use recursive operators, it enqueues the actions to execute instead of executing them right away. A recursive operator is an operator that itself schedules another operator. A good example is repeat. The repeat operator —if given no parameters—keeps repeating the previous Observable sequence in the chain indefinitely.

When to Use It

As a rule of thumb, the queue Scheduler should be used for large sequences and operations that involve recursive operators like repeat, and in general for iterations that contain nested operators.

Scheduling for Animations

For fast visual updates such as canvas or DOM animations, we can either use the interval operator with a extremely low millisecond value or we can make a Scheduler that uses a function like setTimeout internally to schedule notifications.

But neither approach is ideal. In both of them we're throwing all these updates at the browser, which may not be able to process them quickly enough. That happens because the browser is trying to render a frame and then it receives instructions to render the next one, so it drops the current frame to keep up the speed. The result is choppy animations—and there are already enough of those on the web as it is.

Browsers have a native way to handle animations, and they provide an API to use it called requestAnimationFrame. requestAnimationFrame allows the browser to optimize performance by lining up animations at the most appropriate time and helping us achieve smoother animations.

There's a Scheduler for That

RxJS comes with some extra Schedulers, one of which is the animationFrame Scheduler.

Yes, you guessed it. We can use this Scheduler to improve our spaceship video game. In it, we established a refresh speed of 40ms—roughly 25 frames per second—by creating an interval Observable at that speed and then using combineLatest to update the whole game scene at the speed set by interval (because it is the fastest-updating Observable). But who knows how many frames the browser is dropping by using this technique! We would get much better performance by using requestAnimationFrame.

Let's create an Observable that uses Rx.Scheduler.animationFrame as its Scheduler. Notice that it works similarly to how the interval operator works:

ch5/starfield_raf.js
```
function animationLoop() {
  return Observable.generate(
    0,
    () => true,
    x => x + 1,
    x => x,
    Scheduler.animationFrame
  ); // Schedule to requestAnimationFrame
}
```

Now, instead of using interval to animate graphics at 25 FPS, we can just use our animationLoop function. So our Observable to paint stars, which looked like this before:

ch3/spaceship.js
```
const StarStream = Observable.range(1, 250)
  .map(() => ({
    x: parseInt(Math.random() * canvas.width, 10),
    y: parseInt(Math.random() * canvas.height, 10),
    size: Math.random() * 3 + 1
  }))
  .toArray()
  .flatMap(arr =>
    Observable.interval(SPEED).map(() =>
      arr.map(star => {
        if (star.y >= canvas.height) {
          star.y = 0;
        }
        star.y += star.size;
        return star;
      })
    )
  );
```

Becomes this:

ch5/starfield_raf.js
```
const StarStream = Observable
  .range(1, 250)
  .map(() => ({
    x: parseInt(Math.random() * canvas.width),
    y: parseInt(Math.random() * canvas.height),
    size: Math.random() * 3 + 1
  }))
```

```
    .toArray()
➤   .flatMap(arr => animationLoop().map(() =>
    arr.map(star => {
      if (star.y >= canvas.height) {
        star.y = 0;
      }
      star.y += 3;
      return star;
    })));
```

Which gives us a much smoother animation. As a bonus, the code is also cleaner!

Testing with Schedulers

Testing is perhaps one of the most compelling scenarios where we can use Schedulers. So far in this book we've been coding our hearts out without thinking much about the consequences. But in a real-world software project, we would be writing tests to make sure our code works as we intend.

Testing asynchronous code is hard. We usually run into one of these problems:

- Simulating asynchronous events is complicated and error prone. The whole point of having tests is to avoid bugs and errors, but if your tests themselves have errors, they're not helping.

- If we want to accurately test time-based functionality, automated testing becomes really slow. For example, if we need to accurately test that an error is called after four seconds of trying to retrieve a remote file, each test will take at least that much time to run. If we run our test suite continuously, that impacts our development time.

Marble Testing

Marble testing is a new feature in RxJS 5 that allows us to test asynchronous operations in a synchronous and reliable way. The main highlight is that it comes with its own marble-diagram-based domain language that makes it much easier than before to test Observables as shown in the figure on page 96.

Setting It Up

Setting up the tests to be able to use marble testing is a bit cumbersome because the marble testing helpers don't come included in the default distribution of RxJS. Because the original source code is in TypeScript, we can't directly download the helpers file either.

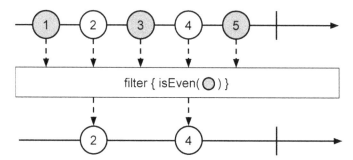

An example marble diagram for the filter operator

The way we do it is by first getting the current RxJS distribution:

```
$ git clone https://github.com/ReactiveX/rxjs.git
Cloning into 'rxjs'...
remote: Counting objects: 30499, done.
remote: Compressing objects: 100% (21/21), done.
remote: Total 30499 (delta 11), reused 4 (delta 4), pack-reused 30474
Receiving objects: 100% (30499/30499), 73.89 MiB | 8.75 MiB/s, done.
Resolving deltas: 100% (23828/23828), done.

$ cd rxjs
$ npm install
...
$ npm run build_all && npm run build_spec
...
```

When this process is finished, you'll find a file named spec-js/helpers/marble-testing.js in the root directory of the project. That's the file we'll import in our tests in order to work with marble syntax.

Using Marble Syntax to Simulate Sequences

Throughout the book we have used marble diagrams to visually represent Observable sequences. Translating those into "marble syntax" is pretty easy. Each sequence is represented by a string of events happening over "time." The first character of any sequence represents the "zero frame." A "frame" is analogous to a virtual millisecond.

The rest of the syntax, from the RxJS source documentation, is shown in table on page 97.

Knowing this syntax, we could write a very simple test in Mocha comparing two Observables that are equal:

Symbol	Meaning	Explanation
-	Time	10 "frames" of time passage
|	Complete	The successful completion of an observable. This is the observable producer signaling complete().
#	Error	An error terminating the observable. This is the observable producer signaling error().
a	Any character	All other characters represent a value being emitted by the producers signaling next().
( )	Sync groupings	When many events need to signal in the same frame synchronously, you can use parentheses to group them. The position of the initial parenthesis determines when it emits its values.
^	Subscription point	Shows the point at which the tested observables will be subscribed to the hot observable. This is the "zero rame" for that observable, every frame before the ^ will be negative (this is relevant only to hot observables).

ch5/marble-testing/src/test.js

```
it("Same marble sequence should pass", () => {
  const testScheduler = new TestScheduler(assert.deepEqual.bind(assert));
  const sequence = "--a--b--|";
  const source = testScheduler.createHotObservable(sequence);

  testScheduler.expectObservable(source).toBe(sequence);
  testScheduler.flush();
});
```

As you can see, we "draw" our Observable streams by using strings. The Observable featured here, for example, emits two items, a and b before ending the Observable. Let's see what happens step by step:

❶ We create a new TestScheduler that compares using Node's assert.deepEqual method. That's because observers generated from TestScheduler are Objects with metadata in them, so we want to do a deep equal instead of just naively comparing them.

❷ The sequence variable is the string representation of the Observable we want to test. It lets two units of time pass, then emits item a, lets two more units of time pass, then emits b, lets two more units of time pass, and then ends the Observable.

❸ We create a "hot" observable by passing sequence to the createHotObservable of the Test Scheduler.

❹ This is the actual test. Using the Test Scheduler expectObservable and toBe methods we can compare the Observable sequence to its string representation. This method will fail if they differ.

❺ We force the testScheduler to execute all the queued actions.

That was a simple example, but hopefully enough to whet your appetite to see how to use this little marble diagram DSL to test more complex scenarios.

A More Realistic Test

Let's make a more realistic test. We will keep our earthquake theme and test whether earthquakes from different sources are merged properly. Here's the code:

ch5/marble-testing/src/test.js
```
it("Should properly merge and exclude earthquakes with magnitude 0", () => {
  const testScheduler = new TestScheduler(assert.deepEqual.bind(assert));
  const quakeMarbles1 = "--b---c--e";
  const quakeMarbles2 = "a------d--";

  const quake1$ = testScheduler.createHotObservable(quakeMarbles1);
  const quake2$ = testScheduler.createHotObservable(quakeMarbles2);

  const expectedValues = {
    a: { richterScale: 2.6 },
    b: { richterScale: 3.4 },
    c: { richterScale: 1.3 },
    d: { richterScale: 0 },
    e: { richterScale: 6.2 }
  };

  const expected = "a-b---c--e";

  const mergedQuakes$ = Observable.merge(quake1$, quake2$)
    .filter(q => q.richterScale && q.richterScale > 0);

  testScheduler
    .expectObservable(mergedQuakes$)
    .toBe(expected, expectedValues);

  testScheduler.flush();
});
```

❶ In this test we handle two Observable sequences, which we represent here using marble syntax.

❷ Just like with the basic test, we create two hot Observables, quake1$ and quake2$, from the Observables expressed in marble syntax.

❸ expectedValues is an object that maps the names of the items emitted by the Observables to their actual values. In our case, the value for each emitted item is an object with a property richterScale, which indicates the magnitude of the Earthquake on the Richter scale. We'll use it in the last step.

❹ This test verifies that both Observable sequences will be merged in the right order, discarding any value of richterScale that is not greater than 0. The expected string is the marble syntax representation of the expected Observable.

❺ Here is where we do the actual merge and filter operations and store it into mergedQuake$.

❻ Our final step is the same as with our basic test from before: we use the expectObservable and toBe methods in testScheduler. There is only one essential difference: in this case, the second argument of toBe is expectedValues.

When we do operations on Observables created from marble syntax strings, we get a single-character string with the name of the emitted item (for example, a, b, c, and so on). In order to map these to the actual values we want to test, we have to create an object (expectedValues) with the names as keys and the desired values. toBe will take care of mapping them properly.

Using marble syntax to test RxJS code is extremely convenient. It saves us a lot of tedious work to set up each Observable sequence, which can be essential when writing complex tests, keeping us from making mistakes when typing the "mock" Observable sequences.

Wrapping Up

Schedulers are an essential part of RxJS. Even if you can go a long way without explicitly using them, they are the advanced concept that will give you the edge to fine-tune concurrency in your programs. The concept of virtual time is unique to RxJS and is incredibly useful for tasks such as testing asynchronous code.

In the next chapter we'll use Cycle.js, a reactive way to create amazing web apps, based on a concept called *unidirectional dataflow*. With it, we'll create a fast web application using modern techniques that improve dramatically on the traditional way of making web apps.

CHAPTER 6

Reactive Web Applications with Cycle.js

With the advent of single-page apps, websites are suddenly expected to do much more—even compete against (gasp!) "native" apps. While trying to make web applications faster, developers realized that particular areas were bottle-necks keeping web applications from being as fast and robust as their native counterparts.

Spearheaded by Facebook React,[1] several web frameworks are coming up with new techniques to make faster web applications while keeping the code simple and declarative.

Web applications such as the Virtual DOM are here to stay, and in this chapter we'll cover some new techniques for developing them. We'll be using Cycle.js, a modern, simple, and beautiful framework that uses RxJS internally and applies reactive programming concepts to front-end programming.

Cycle.js

Cycle.js is a small framework on top of RxJS for creating responsive user interfaces. It offers the features present in modern frameworks like React, such as the Virtual DOM and unidirectional dataflow.

Cycle.js is designed in a reactive way, and all the building blocks in Cycle.js are Observables, which gives us enormous advantages. It is also simpler to grasp than other frameworks because there are far fewer concepts to under-stand and memorize. For example, all operations related to state are out of the way, encapsulated in functions called *drivers*, and we rarely need to create new ones.

---

1. https://facebook.github.io/react/

> ### Joe asks:
> ## What's the Virtual DOM?
>
> The Document Object Model (DOM) defines the tree structure of elements in an HTML document. Every HTML element is a node in the DOM, and each node can be manipulated using methods on the node.
>
> The DOM was originally created to represent static documents, not the super-dynamic websites that we have today. As a consequence, it was not designed to have good performance when the elements in a DOM tree were updated frequently. That's why there's a performance hit when we make changes to the DOM.
>
> The *Virtual DOM* is a representation of the DOM made in JavaScript. Every time we change state in a component, we recompute a new Virtual DOM tree for the component and compare it with the previous tree. If there are differences, we render only those differences. This approach is extremely fast, because comparing JavaScript objects is fast and we make only the absolutely necessary changes to the "real" DOM.
>
> That approach means we can write code as if we generated the whole app UI for every change. We don't have to keep track of state in the DOM. Behind the scenes, Cycle.js will check if there is anything different for every update and take care of rendering our app efficiently.

Installing Cycle.js

We could use Cycle.js by including it in an HTML page using <script></script> tags, but that would not be the best way to use it because Cycle.js is designed in an extremely modular way. Every module tries to be as self-sufficient as possible, and including several modules as scripts could easily load tons of duplicated code, causing unnecessary downloads and longer start-up times for our applications.

Fortunately, the Cycle.js authors have put considerable effort into making good tooling. We are going to depart from our usual configuration and use *create-cycle-app*, a command-line tool that allows you to create Cycle.js apps without having to worry about build configurations, package installations, and the like.

We install create-cycle-app globally using npm:

```
$ npm install -g create-cycle-app
```

And then we use it to create the scaffolding for our application—a Wikipedia Search application:

```
$ create-cycle-app wikipedia-search
Creating a new Cycle.js app in ~/rxjs-book/wikipedia-search.
Installing packages. This might take a couple minutes.
```

This will install a bunch of packages and create a basic configuration for the project. When it's finished, it will present some handy tips about how to run your application, bundle it for production, test it, and so on.

To start the app simply run:

```
$ npm start

> wikipedia-search@0.1.0 start ~/code/smreactjs5/Book/code/cycle/wikipedia-search
> cycle-scripts start

Build completed in 2.138s

App is running at http://localhost:8000

webpack: Compiled successfully
```

This will start the development server and let you know where to find the app. In our case it is http://localhost:8000. For now, there is not much to see there, but we'll change this in the next section!

Our Project: Wikipedia Search

In this section we will build an application that searches Wikipedia as the user types.

RxJS already makes retrieving and processing the remote data easy, but as you saw in Chapter 4, *Building a Complete Web Application*, on page 69, we still need to jump through some hoops to make our DOM operations efficient.

One of the objectives of Cycle.js is to completely eliminate DOM manipulation from our code. Let's look at the generated application code we have so far in src/index.js:

cycle/wikipedia-search/src/index.js

```
① import { run } from "@cycle/run";
   import { makeDOMDriver, div } from "@cycle/dom";
② import { Observable } from 'rxjs'
③ const main = sources => {
④   const vtree$ = Observable.of(
       div('My Awesome Cycle.js app')
     )
⑤   const sinks = {
       DOM: vtree$
     }
     return sinks
   };
⑥ const drivers = {
     DOM: makeDOMDriver("#app")
   };
⑦ run(main, drivers);
```

This code just shows the text *My Awesome Cycle.js app* onscreen, but there's already quite a lot going on. Let's go through the steps:

❶ We start by requiring the functions we'll use. We'll always need run to start a Cycle.js app, and then we require makeDOMDriver and div from the cycle/dom package. We'll explain what these do momentarily, when we use them in the code.

❷ Most likely you didn't have this line in your file, but one that imported xstream instead of RxJS. xstream is an alternative Observable library that was made with Cycle.js in mind, with less operators and targeted to applications that don't use subscribe often. RxJS5 is more complete and entirely "swappable" for xstream to use it with Cycle.js.

❸ The main function returns an object containing a sink for each object key. *Sinks* are sequences of Observables that are sent to *drivers*. In our example, we only have one driver, DOM, specified below in the drivers constant.

❹ The vtree$ Observable emits just one item, a div DOM element with the text 'My Awesome Cycle.js app', created by the helper function div we imported at the top. That div will be the only content in our web page.

❺ This is the sinks object that contains our only sink: DOM. This will be picked up by the DOM driver below.

❻ The drivers object contains a driver for each key. These drivers will listen to the sinks returned by main, matching them by object key.

❼ We finally start the application by calling run and passing our main function and our drivers.

Cycle.js Drivers

Cycle.js drivers are functions we use to cause side effects. Nowhere else in our programs should we be modifying state in any way. Drivers take an Observable that emits data from our application, and they return another Observable that causes the side effects.

We won't be creating drivers very often—only when we need side effects like modifying the DOM, reading and writing from other interfaces (for example, Local Storage), or making requests. In most applications we'll need only the DOM driver (which renders web pages) and the HTTP driver (which we can use to make HTTP requests). In this example, we'll use yet another one, the JSONP driver.

The User Interface

We need actual content for our page, not just a single div. Let's make a function that creates the virtual tree that represents our page:

```
cycle/wikipedia-search/src/index2.js
function vtreeElements(results) {
  return div([
    h1("Wikipedia Search "),
    input({
      className: "search-field",
      attributes: { type: "text" }
    }),
    hr(),
    div(
      results.map(result =>
        div([a({ href: WIKI_URL + result.title }, result.title)])
      )
    )
  ]);
}
```

vtreeElements takes an array of objects, results, and returns a virtual tree that represents the simple UI for our app. It renders an input field and a listing of links made from the objects in results, which eventually will contain Wikipedia's search results. We'll use vtreeElements to render our application.

Using JSX

Instead of using functions like div or h1 to compose our DOM, we could write our UI using JSX, an XML-like syntax extension that makes writing Virtual DOM structures easier and more readable. Our vtreeElements function would look like this:

cycle/wikipedia-search/src/index2.js
```
function vtreeElementsJSX(results) {
  results = results.map(result => {
    var link = WIKI_URL + result.title;
    return (
      <div>
        <a href={link}>{result.title}</a>
      </div>
    );
  });

  return (
    <div>
      <h1>Wikipedia Search</h1>
      <input className="search-field" type="text" />
      <hr />
      <div>{results}</div>
    </div>
  );
}
```

Doesn't it look nicer? JSX looks more familiar to developers because it resembles HTML, but we can write it alongside JavaScript code, with the added advantage that we can treat it as a JavaScript type. For example, notice how we iterate the results array and we return a <div> element directly, using the value of link and result.title in the element itself. (JavaScript values can be inlined by putting them inside curly brackets.)

Setting Up JSX in Our Project

In order to use JSX in our project we need to install the modules *babel-plugin-transform-react-jsx* and *snabbdom-jsx*:

```
‹ npm install --save babel-plugin-transform-react-jsx snabbdom-jsx
```

When the packages are installed, we need to edit the package.json file at the root of our project's folder and add a *"plugins"* section to the *"babel"* property, so that it looks like this:

```
"plugins": [
  "syntax-jsx",
  ["transform-react-jsx", {"pragma": "html"}]
]
```

Next, we can just import Snabbdom JSX in any file using JSX and we'll be set:

```
import {html} from 'snabbdom-jsx';
```

Getting the Search Term from the User

We need a function that returns an Observable of URLs that query Wikipedia's API using search terms entered by the user:

```
cycle/wikipedia-search/src/index2.js
const MAIN_URL = "https://en.wikipedia.org";
const WIKI_URL = `${MAIN_URL}/wiki/`;
const API_URL = `${MAIN_URL}/w/api.php?` +
  `action=query&list=search&format=json&srsearch=`;

function searchRequest(responses) {
  return responses.DOM
    .map(".search-field")
    .events("input")
    .debounceTime(300)
    .map(e => e.target.value)
    .filter(value => value.length > 2)
    .map(search => API_URL + search);
}
```

First we declare some URLs our application will use to query Wikipedia. In the function searchRequest we take a responses object that contains all the drivers in our application, and we use the get method in the DOM driver. select(element).event(type) behaves similarly to fromEvent: it takes a selector for a DOM element and the type of event to listen to and returns an Observable that emits events.

From that moment on, the rest of the code should look familiar to you, since it consists of transforming an Observable's values through our usual operators:

❶ Throttle results to receive one every 300 milliseconds at most.

❷ Extract the value of the input box.

❸ Take only text longer than two characters.

❹ Append the final value to Wikipedia's API URL.

Great! So far we have the function to generate our UI and the function to retrieve user input from that UI. We now need to add the functionality that will get the information from Wikipedia.

Revising Our main Function

You may have noticed in the code on page 104 that the main function takes a parameter, sources, that we're not using. These are the messages that come from drivers in the run function. The drivers and the main function form a cycle (hence the name of the framework): the output of main is the input of the drivers, and the output of the drivers is the input for main. And remember, inputs and outputs are always Observables.

We use JSONP to query Wikipedia, as we did in Chapter 2, *Deep in the Sequence*, on page 17. We are using JSONP instead of HTTP to make it easier to run this example on our local computer, since retrieving data from a different domain using HTTP causes some browsers to block those requests for security reasons. In almost any other situation, especially in production code, use HTTP to retrieve remote data.

In any case, using JSONP doesn't affect the point of this chapter. Cycle has an experimental module for JSONP, and we can install it using npm:

```
npm install @cycle/jsonp
```

Then we use it in our application like this:

cycle/wikipedia-search/src/step2.js
```
import { run } from "@cycle/run";
import { makeDOMDriver, div, h1, input, hr, a } from "@cycle/dom";
import { Observable } from "rxjs";
import makeJSONPDriver from "@cycle/jsonp";

const MAIN_URL = "https://en.wikipedia.org";
const WIKI_URL = `${MAIN_URL}/wiki/`;
const API_URL = `${MAIN_URL}/w/api.php?action=query&list=search&format=json&srsearch=`;

function searchRequest(responses) {
  return responses.DOM
    .map(".search-field")
    .events("input")
    .debounceTime(300)
    .map(e => e.target.value)
    .filter(value => value.length > 2)
    .map(search => API_URL + search);
}

function vtreeElements(results) {
  results = results.map(result => {
    const link = WIKI_URL + result.title;
    return (
      <div>
        <a href={link}>{result.title}</a>
      </div>
    );
  });

  return (
    <div>
```

```
          <h1>Wikipedia Search</h1>
          <input className="search-field" type="text" />
          <hr />
          <div>{results}</div>
        </div>
      );
    }

    const main = sources => {
      const vtree$ = Observable.of(div("My Awesome Cycle.js app"));
      const sinks = {
        DOM: vtree$,
➤       JSONP: searchRequest(sources)
      };
      return sinks;
    };

    const drivers = {
      DOM: makeDOMDriver("#app"),
➤     JSONP: makeJSONPDriver()
    };

    run(main, drivers);
```

We want to plug the result of searchRequest into the JSONP driver, so that as soon as the user types a search term, we query Wikipedia with the term.

To do that, we create a new JSONP driver using CycleJSONP.makeJSONPDriver, which will receive whatever we put in the property JSONP in the return object from main. After doing that, we should already be querying Wikipedia when we introduce a search term in the input box, but since we're not connecting the JSONP output to anything, we don't see any changes on the page. Let's change that:

cycle/step3.js
```
function main(responses) {
  var vtree$ = responses.JSONP
❶   .filter(res$ => res$.request.indexOf(API_URL) === 0)
❷   .mergeAll()
❸   .pluck('query', 'search')
❹   .startWith([])
❺   .map(vtreeElements);

  return {
    DOM: vtree$,
    JSONP: searchRequest(responses)
  };
}
```

main receives the output of all drivers through its responses parameter. We can get the result of the JSON calls in sources.JSONP, an Observable of all the JSONP responses in our application. Once we have that, we can transform the Observable to get the search results in the form we want:

❶ sources.JSONP emits all JSONP responses in the application. We start by filtering by the ones that contain the API URL of Wikipedia in its request, to make sure that we're processing the relevant responses.

❷ sources.JSONP is an Observable of Observables. For each source there is an Observable. In this line we flatten them all out, so we deal with the sources themselves from now on, instead of their Observables.

The sources are JSON objects, and the information we're interested in is in the query.search property. We use the pluck operator to extract it.

❸ We don't know if we'll have any results, so at the very least we ensure we'll have an empty array.

❹ Finally, we apply our vtreeElements function to every result from Wikipedia. This will update our UI.

❺ Notice the $ sign at the end of the variable's name. In this chapter I'm adopting a naming convention used in Cycle.js code that adds $ to the name of a variable to mean that it is an Observable. I found that it makes it much easier to understand Observable-based code!

The most important takeaway from the preceding code is that in the last step we seem to be repainting the whole UI for every single result that we receive. But here's where the Virtual DOM shines. No matter how many times we re-render the page, the Virtual DOM will always ensure that only the differences are rendered, making it very efficient. If there are no changes to the Virtual DOM, no changes will be rendered in the page.

This way we don't have to worry about adding or removing elements. We just render the whole application every time, and we let the Virtual DOM figure out what to actually update under the hood.

Model-View-Intent

The architectural approach we used to build the Wikipedia real-time search is not just another framework's random approach to programming UI. There's a design pattern behind structuring code like we did: *Model-View-Intent* (MVI).

Model-View-Intent is a term coined by the creator of Cycle.js, André Staltz, for an architecture inspired by the Model-View-Controller (MVC) pattern.[2] In

---

2. https://en.wikipedia.org/wiki/Model-view-controller

MVC we separate the functionality of an application into three components: the model, the view, and the controller. In MVI, the three components are the model, the view, and the intent. MVI is designed to fit the Reactive model of programming like a glove.

MVI being reactive means that each component observes its dependencies and reacts to the dependencies' changes. This is different from MVC, in which a component knows its dependents and modifies them directly. A component (C) *declares* which other components influence it, instead of other components updating (C) explicitly.

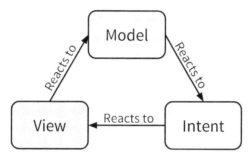

The three components in MVI are represented by Observables, the output of each being the input of another component.

The *model* represents the current application state. It takes processed user input from the *intent* and it outputs events about data changes that are consumed by the *view*.

The view is a visual representation of our model. It takes an Observable with the model state, and it outputs all the potential DOM events and the virtual tree of the page.

The intent is the new component in MVI. An intent takes input from the user and translates it to actions in our model.

We can make the three kinds of components more clear in our application if we reshuffle and rename our code a bit:

cycle/index-mvi.js
```
function intent(JSONP) {
  return JSONP.filter(res$ => res$.request.indexOf(API_URL) === 0)
    .concatAll()
    .pluck("query", "search");
}

function model(actions) {
  return actions.startWith([]);
}
```

```
function view(state) {
  return state.map(linkArray =>
    h("div", [
      h("h1", "Wikipedia Search "),
      h("input", {
        className: "search-field",
        attributes: { type: "text" }
      }),
      h("hr"),
      h(
        "div",
        linkArray.map(link =>
          h("div", [h("a", { href: WIKI_URL + link.title }, link.title)])
        )
      )
    ])
  );
}

function userIntent(DOM) {
  return DOM.map(".search-field")
    .events("input")
    .debounceTime(300)
    .map(e => e.target.value)
    .filter(value => value.length > 2)
    .map(search => API_URL + search);
}

function main(responses) {
  return {
    DOM: view(model(intent(responses.JSONP))),
    JSONP: userIntent(responses.DOM)
  };
}
run(main, {
  DOM: makeDOMDriver("#container"),
  JSONP: makeJSONPDriver()
});
```

By splitting the model, view, and intent into separate functions, we make the code much clearer. (The other intent, userIntent, is the input for the JSONP driver.) Most of the appplication logic is expressed as a composition of these three functions in the property we pass to the DOM driver in the main function:

```
function main(responses) {
  return {
➤    DOM: view(model(intent(responses.JSONP))),
    JSONP: userIntent(responses.DOM)
  };
}
```

It doesn't get much more functional than that!

Creating Reusable Widgets

As we make more complex applications, we'll want to reuse some of their UI components. Our Wikipedia Search application is tiny for the sake of example, but it already has a couple of components that could be reused in other applications. Take the search input box, for example. We can definitely make this into its own widget.

The objective is to encapsulate our widget in its own component so that we use it as any other DOM element. We should also be able to parameterize the component with any properties we want. Then we'll use it in our applications like this:

```
var wpSearchBox = searchBox({
  props$: Rx.Observable.just({
    apiUrl: API_URL
  })
});
```

We'll build our widget using a concept also introduced by Cycle.js, called *nested dialogues*. A nested dialogue, or *dialogue*, is a function (like everything in Cycle.js) that takes an Observable of events as input, and outputs an Observable—with the result of applying these inputs to its internal logic.

Let's start building the search-box component. We first create a function that takes a responses parameter where we'll pass it any properties we want from the main application:

```
cycle/searchbox.js
import { h } from "@cycle/dom";
import { Observable } from "rxjs";

function searchBox(responses) {
  const props$ = responses.props$;
  const apiUrl$ = props$.map(props => props["apiUrl"]).first();
```

Every parameter searchBox receives is an Observable. In this case props$ is an Observable that emits a single JavaScript object containing the configuration parameters for our Wikipedia search box.

After retrieving the properties, we define the virtual tree for our widget. In our case, it is a very simple one that contains just an input field:

```
cycle/searchbox.js
const vtree$ = Observable.of(
  h("div", { className: "search-field" }, [h("input", { type: "text" })])
);
```

We want everything to be an Observable, so we wrapped the virtual tree in an of Observable, which returns an Observable that emits the value we pass it.

Now we need the search box to query the Wikipedia API whenever the user types a search term in the input field. We reuse the code in the function userIntent from our previous section:

cycle/searchbox.js
```
const searchQuery$ = apiUrl$.flatMap(apiUrl =>
  responses.DOM
    .map(".search-field")
    .events("input")
    .debounceTime(300)
    .map(e => e.target.value)
    .filter(value => value.length > 3)
    .map(searchTerm => apiUrl + searchTerm)
);
```

We still need to connect the output of searchQuery to the input of the JSON driver. We do that just like we do it in the normal Cycle application:

cycle/searchbox.js
```
return {
  DOMTree: vtree$,
  JSONPQuery: searchQuery$
};
```

And finally, we shouldn't forget to export the searchBox widget:

cycle/searchbox.js
```
module.exports = searchBox; // Export it as a module
```

Now we're ready to use the searchBox widget in our application. The main method will now look like this:

cycle/index-mvi2.js
```
const SearchBox = require("./searchbox");

function main(responses) {
  const wpSearchBox = SearchBox({
    DOM: responses.DOM,
    props$: Observable.of({
      apiUrl: API_URL
    })
  });

  const searchDOM$ = wpSearchBox.DOMTree;
  const searchResults$ = responses.JSONP
    .filter(res$ => res$.request.indexOf(API_URL) === 0)
    .concatAll()
    .pluck("query", "search")
    .startWith([]);
```

```
    return {
      JSONP: wpSearchBox.JSONPQuery,
      DOM: Observable.combineLatest(searchDOM$, searchResults$, (
        tree,
        links
      ) =>
        h("div", [
          h("h1", "Wikipedia Search "),
          tree,
          h("hr"),
          h(
            "div",
            links.map(link =>
              h("div", [h("a", { href: WIKI_URL + link.title }, link.title)])
            )
          )
        ])
      )
    };
}

run(main, {
  DOM: makeDOMDriver("#container"),
  JSONP: makeJSONPDriver()
});
```

Now we delegate the responsibility of handling user input and rendering the search box to the wpSearchBox widget, which we could easily reuse in another application that requires a search box that queries URL APIs. These are the main changes:

❶ Import the searchBox widget we just created.

❷ Create an instance of SearchBox, passing the DOM driver and the properties we want for our search widget.

❸ Our wpSearchBox will eventually emit items from its DOMTree Observable. We assign it here to use them later when we render the actual DOM.

❹ We send the Wikipedia query URLs to the JSONP driver so that it retrieves its results. When those are available, it will emit them in response.JSONP, which we refine in searchResults.

❺ To render the final DOM tree, we use combineLatest with searchDOM and searchResults. Each of them causes the layout to change, so we'll re-render the DOM tree whenever one of these two Observables emits an item.

With the final code in hand, we can see the greatest point of Cycle.js. There are no different classes, special types, or "magic" happening in the framework.

It's all side effect–free functions that accept Observables and output more Observables. With only that, we have a concise web application framework that is clear, reactive, and fun to use. And it avoids side effects at all costs, making our web applications more robust.

Ideas for Improvements

Besides being in urgent need of a better graphical design, our application could use some features to be more than a quick redirect to Wikipedia results:

- Let the user bookmark particular results. You could add a little star next to every result in the list so that when the user clicks, it saves that result as a favorite. You could make the star into its own widget. Extra points if you use some persistent API (reactively!), such as Local Storage or IndexedDB.

- Show a "preview" of a result on the right side of the screen if the user clicks the link, with a synopsis and some meta information about it. If the user wants to go to the actual Wikipedia result, you can have a "Read More" link in it. Implement it as a widget.

Wrapping Up

Now you know how to develop web applications that use modern techniques without abandoning the reactive philosophy. This chapter provided an idea of how to use Observables and RxJS as the internal engine of other frameworks or applications. By standing on the shoulders of Observables and the reactive way of life, we can enormously simplify web applications and reduce state to its minimum expression, making our web applications less fragile and more maintainable.

Thank you for reading this book. I hope it helped you rethink the way you develop JavaScript applications, and challenged some of your existing concepts about programming. Here's to fast, robust, and reactive software!

Index

Thank you!

How did you enjoy this book? Please let us know. Take a moment and email us at support@pragprog.com with your feedback. Tell us your story and you could win free ebooks. Please use the subject line "Book Feedback."

Ready for your next great Pragmatic Bookshelf book? Come on over to https://pragprog.com and use the coupon code BUYANOTHER2017 to save 30% on your next ebook.

Void where prohibited, restricted, or otherwise unwelcome. Do not use ebooks near water. If rash persists, see a doctor. Doesn't apply to *The Pragmatic Programmer* ebook because it's older than the Pragmatic Bookshelf itself. Side effects may include increased knowledge and skill, increased marketability, and deep satisfaction. Increase dosage regularly.

And thank you for your continued support,

Andy Hunt, Publisher

SAVE 30%!
Use coupon code
BUYANOTHER2017

The Modern Web

Get up to speed on the latest HTML, CSS, and JavaScript techniques, and secure your Node applications.

HTML5 and CSS3 (2nd edition)

HTML5 and CSS3 are more than just buzzwords – they're the foundation for today's web applications. This book gets you up to speed on the HTML5 elements and CSS3 features you can use right now in your current projects, with backwards compatible solutions that ensure that you don't leave users of older browsers behind. This new edition covers even more new features, including CSS animations, IndexedDB, and client-side validations.

Brian P. Hogan
(314 pages) ISBN: 9781937785598. $38
https://pragprog.com/book/bhh52e

Secure Your Node.js Web Application

Cyber-criminals have your web applications in their crosshairs. They search for and exploit common security mistakes in your web application to steal user data. Learn how you can secure your Node.js applications, database and web server to avoid these security holes. Discover the primary attack vectors against web applications, and implement security best practices and effective countermeasures. Coding securely will make you a stronger web developer and analyst, and you'll protect your users.

Karl Düüna
(230 pages) ISBN: 9781680500851. $36
https://pragprog.com/book/kdnodesec

Level Up

From data structures to architecture and design, we have what you need.

A Common-Sense Guide to Data Structures and Algorithms

If you last saw algorithms in a university course or at a job interview, you're missing out on what they can do for your code. Learn different sorting and searching techniques, and when to use each. Find out how to use recursion effectively. Discover structures for specialized applications, such as trees and graphs. Use Big O notation to decide which algorithms are best for your production environment. Beginners will learn how to use these techniques from the start, and experienced developers will rediscover approaches they may have forgotten.

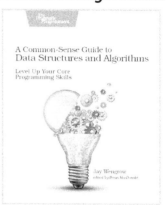

Jay Wengrow
(218 pages) ISBN: 9781680502442. $45.95
https://pragprog.com/book/jwdsal

Design It!

Don't engineer by coincidence—design it like you mean it! Grounded by fundamentals and filled with practical design methods, this is the perfect introduction to software architecture for programmers who are ready to grow their design skills. Ask the right stakeholders the right questions, explore design options, share your design decisions, and facilitate collaborative workshops that are fast, effective, and fun. Become a better programmer, leader, and designer. Use your new skills to lead your team in implementing software with the right capabilities—and develop awesome software!

Michael Keeling
(358 pages) ISBN: 9781680502091. $41.95
https://pragprog.com/book/mkdsa

Data Science and Python

For data science and basic science, for you and anyone else on your team.

Data Science Essentials in Python

Go from messy, unstructured artifacts stored in SQL and NoSQL databases to a neat, well-organized dataset with this quick reference for the busy data scientist. Understand text mining, machine learning, and network analysis; process numeric data with the NumPy and Pandas modules; describe and analyze data using statistical and network-theoretical methods; and see actual examples of data analysis at work. This one-stop solution covers the essential data science you need in Python.

Dmitry Zinoviev
(224 pages) ISBN: 9781680501841. $29
https://pragprog.com/book/dzpyds

Practical Programming, Third Edition

Classroom-tested by tens of thousands of students, this new edition of the best-selling intro to programming book is for anyone who wants to understand computer science. Learn about design, algorithms, testing, and debugging. Discover the fundamentals of programming with Python 3.6—a language that's used in millions of devices. Write programs to solve real-world problems, and come away with everything you need to produce quality code. This edition has been updated to use the new language features in Python 3.6.

Paul Gries, Jennifer Campbell, Jason Montojo
(410 pages) ISBN: 9781680502688. $49.95
https://pragprog.com/book/gwpy3

Explore Testing

Explore the uncharted waters of exploratory testing and delve deeper into web testing.

Explore It!

Uncover surprises, risks, and potentially serious bugs with exploratory testing. Rather than designing all tests in advance, explorers design and execute small, rapid experiments, using what they learned from the last little experiment to inform the next. Learn essential skills of a master explorer, including how to analyze software to discover key points of vulnerability, how to design experiments on the fly, how to hone your observation skills, and how to focus your efforts.

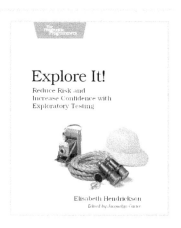

Elisabeth Hendrickson
(186 pages) ISBN: 9781937785024. $29
https://pragprog.com/book/ehxta

The Way of the Web Tester

This book is for everyone who needs to test the web. As a tester, you'll automate your tests. As a developer, you'll build more robust solutions. And as a team, you'll gain a vocabulary and a means to coordinate how to write and organize automated tests for the web. Follow the testing pyramid and level up your skills in user interface testing, integration testing, and unit testing. Your new skills will free you up to do other, more important things while letting the computer do the one thing it's really good at: quickly running thousands of repetitive tasks.

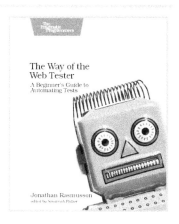

Jonathan Rasmusson
(256 pages) ISBN: 9781680501834. $29
https://pragprog.com/book/jrtest

Seven in Seven

From Web Frameworks to Concurrency Models, see what the rest of the world is doing with this introduction to seven different approaches.

Seven Web Frameworks in Seven Weeks

Whether you need a new tool or just inspiration, *Seven Web Frameworks in Seven Weeks* explores modern options, giving you a taste of each with ideas that will help you create better apps. You'll see frameworks that leverage modern programming languages, employ unique architectures, live client-side instead of server-side, or embrace type systems. You'll see everything from familiar Ruby and JavaScript to the more exotic Erlang, Haskell, and Clojure.

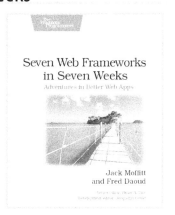

Jack Moffitt, Fred Daoud
(302 pages) ISBN: 9781937785635. $38
https://pragprog.com/book/7web

Seven Concurrency Models in Seven Weeks

Your software needs to leverage multiple cores, handle thousands of users and terabytes of data, and continue working in the face of both hardware and software failure. Concurrency and parallelism are the keys, and *Seven Concurrency Models in Seven Weeks* equips you for this new world. See how emerging technologies such as actors and functional programming address issues with traditional threads and locks development. Learn how to exploit the parallelism in your computer's GPU and leverage clusters of machines with MapReduce and Stream Processing. And do it all with the confidence that comes from using tools that help you write crystal clear, high-quality code.

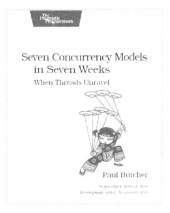

Paul Butcher
(296 pages) ISBN: 9781937785659. $38
https://pragprog.com/book/pb7con

The Pragmatic Bookshelf

The Pragmatic Bookshelf features books written by developers for developers. The titles continue the well-known Pragmatic Programmer style and continue to garner awards and rave reviews. As development gets more and more difficult, the Pragmatic Programmers will be there with more titles and products to help you stay on top of your game.

Visit Us Online

This Book's Home Page
https://pragprog.com/book/smreactjs5
Source code from this book, errata, and other resources. Come give us feedback, too!

Register for Updates
https://pragprog.com/updates
Be notified when updates and new books become available.

Join the Community
https://pragprog.com/community
Read our weblogs, join our online discussions, participate in our mailing list, interact with our wiki, and benefit from the experience of other Pragmatic Programmers.

New and Noteworthy
https://pragprog.com/news
Check out the latest pragmatic developments, new titles and other offerings.

Save on the eBook

Save on the eBook versions of this title. Owning the paper version of this book entitles you to purchase the electronic versions at a terrific discount.

PDFs are great for carrying around on your laptop—they are hyperlinked, have color, and are fully searchable. Most titles are also available for the iPhone and iPod touch, Amazon Kindle, and other popular e-book readers.

Buy now at *https://pragprog.com/coupon*

Contact Us

Online Orders:	*https://pragprog.com/catalog*
Customer Service:	*support@pragprog.com*
International Rights:	*translations@pragprog.com*
Academic Use:	*academic@pragprog.com*
Write for Us:	*http://write-for-us.pragprog.com*
Or Call:	+1 800-699-7764

Lightning Source UK Ltd.
Milton Keynes UK
UKHW051122200922
409142UK00007B/1414